TV'S GREATEST HITS
QUIZ BOOK

ANTHONY DAVIS

First published in Great Britain in 1989
by Boxtree Limited

Copyright © Boxtree Limited 1989

Typeset by Cambrian Typesetters, Frimley, Surrey.
Printed and bound in Great Britain by
Richard Clay Plc, Bungay, Suffolk.

For Boxtree Limited
36 Tavistock Street
London
WC2E 7PB

Cover design by Head Productions

British Library Cataloguing in Publication Data
Davis, Anthony, *1927–*
   T.V.'s greatest hits quiz book.
   1. Great Britain.   Television programmes   2. United
States. Television programmes
I. Title
791.45'0941

ISBN 1–85283–261–4

Contents

Foreword

The Avengers, *Bonanza* and *Dr Kildare*; *The Saint*, *The World at War* and *M*A*S*H* are all very different types of series but they have at least one thing in common. Subtitled or dubbed in foreign languages, they have crossed frontiers and have been seen in most countries of the world.

They are some of television's most successful programmes and continue to be seen – as do others in the same category. The opening of new TV channels, and satellite and cable networks, and the extension of broadcasting hours through the day and night, have meant an increased demand for programmes on film and videotape, and a new lease of life for old programmes. Consequently countless viewers who were not born when *The Lone Ranger* and *Sergeant Bilko* were first screened in the Fifties have seen them in re-runs.

These series are among *TV's Greatest Hits*, which I surveyed in a hardback book of that title also published by Boxtree. This quiz compendium is based upon those programmes and their stars. Some of the questions are intended to be easy and some difficult – though what may confound a casual viewer of a series can be elementary to a fan.

The aim of this book is two-fold: to provide a chance to test your knowledge of television's most popular series, and to stimulate memories of hours spent viewing them.

Anthony Davis

Openers

1. In which British series did Edward Woodward star as a secret service agent 18 years before *The Equalizer*?

2. A woman character in *Gunsmoke* got through 900 shots of whisky and 365 glasses of beer, and smashed 27 bottles over the heads of objectionable men. Who was she?

3. Who was Jim Rockford's broken-nosed policeman pal (played by Joe Santos) in *The Rockford Files*?

4. Of which American TV superhero did Russia's *Pravda* say: 'He is nothing more than a glorified FBI agent, a capitalist murderer'?

5. Which short-lived dance craze was launched by *Batman*?

6. Which soap star has daughters named Tara, Sacha and Katyana?

7. The first owner of the Shiloh ranch in *The Virginian* was Judge Henry Garth. Who was the second?

8. Cybill Shepherd of *Moonlighting* was formerly a model. In which year was she named 'Model of the Year'?

9. Her partner, Bruce Willis, was raised in New Jersey, but in which country was he born?

10. Which glamorous woman star of a police series said: 'I dress for women, and undress for men'?

11. Which *Coronation Street* character is famous for her unusual earrings?

12. After crashing on an unknown planet in *Lost in Space*, the astronauts found a pet – a cross between a puppy, a monkey and a teddy bear. What did they call it?

13. *Voyage to the Bottom of the Sea* was made in 1964 and featured 'Seaview', a submarine of the future. In which year was it set?

14. In which action series did Boy George make his American TV debut in an episode called *Cowboy George*?

Answers on page 79.

Laughtermakers

1. There was trouble at a penitentiary in California when the local TV station switched *The Benny Hill Show* to 11.30 p.m. Why?

2. Hill called himself Benny after Jack Benny. What is his real name?

3. What was Hill's first movie in 1956 in which he played an ice rink sweeper?

4. What name is given to *The Benny Hill Show*'s dance troupe?

5. What musical instrument did Jack Benny play?

6. What was his main characteristic – according to his own jokes?

7. Who was the wife and TV partner of George Burns?

8. Rowan and Martin's *Laugh-In* starred Dick Martin and Dan Rowan. Which was the straight man?

9. Who was the *Laugh-In* actress who played a switch-board operator inquiring, 'Is this the party to whom I am speaking?'

10. Who wore a German steel helmet, lurked behind a potted plant and sneered, 'Verry interesting . . . but stupid'?

11. Who was the English actress who usually said the line, 'Sock it to me' and was then subjected to indignities?

12. Every show opened with announcer Gary Owens, hand cupped to ear, declaring, what?

13. What is the name of the occasional series in which Denis Norden strings together gaffes and duff film out-takes from TV and movies?

14. What do Americans call such shows?

15. Who was Norden's long-time comedy scriptwriting partner?

Answers on page 79.

Secret Agents

1. In *I Spy*, Robert Culp and Bill Cosby played undercover men who travelled the world. What were their respective cover roles?

2. In *Mission Impossible* what was the particular expertise of Rollin Hand (Martin Landau)?

3. Who was the character played by Landau's wife, Barbara Bain?

4. Every week the head of the force received instructions on a tape. What were always the last words on the tape?

5. *The Champions* featured three agents, two men and a woman, Sharron Macready. Who played her?

6. Where, and in what circumstances were *The Champions* given their remarkable powers and heightened senses?

7. What could *The Champions* not do?

8. In *Department S*, Peter Wyngarde played a crime novelist who later featured in a series under his own name. What was it?

9. Who was the hero of his thrillers?

10. *The Six Million Dollar Man* was based on a book by Martin Caidin. What was it called?

11. What was the name of the hero, played by Lee Majors?

12. He was reconstructed after a plane crash. Which of his limbs and organs were replaced?

13. What was the name of *The Bionic Woman*, his girlfriend played by Lindsay Wagner?

14. Who played George Cowley, boss of *The Professionals*?

15. In which action movie did Lewis Collins star as a result of playing Bodie in *The Professionals*?

Answers on page 79.

Bonanza

1. Who was the actor who played Ben, the head of the Cartwright family?

2. What nationality was the actor?

3. How many sons had Ben Cartwright?

4. What relation to each other were Ben Cartwright's sons?

5. Who played the oldest son, Adam, and was the first star to leave the series?

6. Which big star of the series died in 1972 while it was still in production?

7. Which star, who stayed to the end, went on to play Charlie Ingalls?

8. What was the given first name of the Cartwright known as 'Hoss'?

9. What role was played by David Canary?

10. At the height of *Bonanza*'s popularity a number of homes in England were named after the ranch. What was the name?

11. The ranch was supposedly in Nevada – near which city?

12. It was in the middle of the Comstock Lode, site of a valuable metal deposit. Of which metal?

13. Who were played by Geraldine Brooks, Inga Swenson and Felicia Farr?

14. What was the name of Little Joe's horse?

15. *Bonanza* influenced another series, in which Barbara Stanwyck played a matriarchal cattle rancher. What was it?

Answers on page 79.

Trouble Shooters

1. What was the name of *The Saint*?

2. What was the registration number of his car?

3. Who was the Saint's policeman adversary?

4. Roger Moore starred in the original series; who starred in *The Return of the Saint*?

5. What was the name of *The Baron*?

6. The Baron was a shop owner; what did his shops sell?

7. The Baron was played by Steve Forrest, younger brother of which film star?

8. Who was the best-selling author who created The Baron?

9. In *Man in a Suitcase* Richard Bradford played a modern bounty hunter known only by his surname. What was it?

10. What was the name of the character played by Roger Moore in *The Persuaders*?

11. Who was his American co-star?

12. Who starred in *The Adventurer* as film star Gene Bradley?

13. Who was the character played by Lee Majors in *The Fall Guy*?

14. In *The A-Team*, Mr T played B. A. Baracus. What did B. A. stand for?

15. Of what was he afraid?

16. What was the name of the character played by Edward Woodward in *The Equalizer*?

Answers on page 80.

Author! Author!

Who wrote the books on which these series, or mini-series, were based?

1. *The Thorn Birds.*
2. *Princess Daisy.*
3. *Lace.*
4. *Sins.*
5. *Hollywood Wives.*
6. *Wheels.*
7. *The Saint.*
8. *The Rhinemann Exchange.*
9. *79 Park Avenue.*
10. *The Immigrants.*
11. *The Winds of War.*
12. *North and South.*
13. *Shogun.*
14. *The Pallisers.*
15. *Anna Karenina.*
16. *Tender is the Night.*
17. *Poldark.*
18. *Seventh Avenue.*
19. *Evening in Byzantium.*
20. *Captains and the Kings.*

Answers on page 80.

American Peepers

1. Who was the insurance company detective (played by George Peppard) hailed as 'television's first Polish-American hero'?

2. William Conrad had few television parts before *Cannon* because of his bulk, but he played a role on American radio for 11 years. What was it?

3. James Garner quit *The Rockford Files* after six years, complaining of injuries suffered in falls and leaps. Which part of his body had he hurt?

4. Where in his home did Rockford keep his gun?

5. In which war was James Garner wounded and decorated with the Purple Heart?

6. Who was the actor, later a star of *Dynasty*, who provided the voice of the unseen Charlie in *Charlie's Angels*?

7. What was the name of the computerised security firm for which *Mannix* worked?

8. *Magnum* was known to his friends as 'T. S.'. For what did the initials stand?

9. For what offence was *Mike Hammer* star Stacy Keach imprisoned in England, causing a headline, 'Hammer in the Slammer'?

10. When not playing detectives in *Hart to Hart*, Jonathan Hart was a businessman. What was Mrs Hart's profession?

11. Who were the characters of *The Thin Man* films of the Thirties, starring William Powell and Myrna Loy, that the Harts were devised to emulate?

12. Edd Byrnes, who played the car park attendant in *77 Sunset Strip*, made a hit record with Connie Stevens. What was its title?

13. Much of the action in *77 Sunset Strip* took place outside whose restaurant?

Answers on page 80.

Nicknames

Who were the characters who bore these nicknames, and what were the series in which they appeared?

1. Potsie.

2. Triple A.

3. Pepper.

4. Kookie.

5. The Fonz.

6. Melonhead.

7. Hawkeye.

8. Hot Lips.

9. The Faceman.

10. Pug.

11. Digger.

12. Dandy Jim.

13. Bones.

14. Tickler.

15. Rocky.

Answers on page 80.

Tales Of The Raj

1. In *The Far Pavilions* who played the British officer, Ash, escorting two Indian princesses to their weddings?

2. What was the name of his elite regiment?

3. What was the name of the princess, played by Amy Irving, who was the officer's childhood sweetheart?

4. Who wrote the book, *The Far Pavilions*?

5. A rape in public gardens triggered events in *The Jewel in the Crown*. Who was the victim?

6. What was the name of the gardens?

7. What was the job of Hari Kumar who was accused of the crime?

8. Who was the keeper of the Sanctuary, the mission where Kumar was arrested?

9. Who was the ex-missionary played by Dame Peggy Ashcroft?

10. Tim Pigott-Smith became a star as a sneering police superintendant, later an Indian Army officer, in *The Jewel in the Crown*. What was the character's name?

11. What were the rank and unit of Guy Perron (Charles Dance)?

12. Of which public school was he an Old Boy?

13. What was the post of Count Bronowsky, the Russian played by Eric Porter?

14. Warren Clarke played the camp Corporal Dixon of the Army Medical Corps. By what name was Dixon known?

15. *The Jewel in the Crown* was based on the Raj Quartet of novels. By whom were these written?

Answers on page 81.

The Fugitive

1. David Janssen played *The Fugitive*; what was the character's name?

2. What was the French novel about a man on the run that inspired *The Fugitive*?

3. The Fugitive was convicted of murdering his wife; what was the sentence?

4. What accident enabled him to escape from custody?

5. What was the first name of his murdered wife, seen in flashbacks?

6. What was the name of the police lieutenant, played by Barry Morse, who pursued the Fugitive?

7. The Fugitive had only one relative with whom he kept in touch while on the run. Who?

8. How many years did the manhunt (and the TV series) last?

9. What was the association between the Fugitive and men named Corbin, Fowler, Lincoln, McGuire, Owen, Russell and Wallace?

10. What was the link between *The Fugitive* and *Cannon*.

11. At the end, the Fugitive cornered the one-armed man on the top of a tower in an amusement park and they fought. How did the fight end?

12. What was the name of the one-armed man, played by one-armed actor Bill Raisch?

13. David Janssen went on to play a private detective in *Harry O*. For what did the 'O' stand?

14. Morse went on to play a mysterious government agent named Parminter in a British espionage series. What was it?

15. *The Fugitive* production team went on to make another series about a man on the run – this time from alien creatures. What was it called?

Answers on page 81.

Legendary Heroes

1. Who starred in *The Adventures of Robin Hood*, made in 1955?

2. Paul Eddington, since famous for *Yes, Prime Minister*, played one of the outlaws. Which one?

3. Two actresses played Maid Marian in the course of the series. Who were they?

4. Real chain mail armour was too heavy for the actors. What was used instead?

5. The theme song was ITV's first musical hit. Who was the singer?

6. What was the title of the BBC Robin Hood series in 1977 with Martin Potter as the outlaw?

7. And the HTV series in 1984 with Michael Praed (succeeded by Jason Connery)?

8. Who played the title role in *The Adventures of Sir Lancelot*?

9. *Tarzan* was an English aristocrat. What was his full title?

10. Who played *Tarzan* on TV in the Sixties?

11. What was the name of his chimp friend?

12. Who was the orphaned jungle boy played by Manuel Padilla Jr?

13. Who wrote the *Tarzan* books?

14. What was the name of the half-Chinese, half-American played by David Carradine in *Kung Fu*?

15. In which Western series did Carradine star earlier?

Answers on page 81.

Kookie Talk

Kookie, the car park attendant who became a private eye in *77 Sunset Strip*, spoke a language of his own. Can you interpret these phrases of his?

1. Out of print.
2. Buzzed by germsville.
3. Headache grapplers.
4. Pile up the z's.
5. Drum beaters.
6. Wheel-spinning.
7. Cut your motor.
8. Let's exitville.
9. Keep the eyes rolling.
10. Real nervous.
11. Making the long green.
12. Pony chaser.
13. Tintype.
14. Go the minnow route.
15. Ride the straws.

Answers on page 81.

The First TV Cops

1. Who was the actor who devised, wrote, produced and starred as Sgt Joe Friday in *Dragnet*?

2. What was Friday's badge number?

3. In which city was *Dragnet* set?

4. The closing announcement every week said that the stories were true but names had been changed. Why?

5. *Dragnet* rationed shootings; how frequently were they permitted?

6. Who recorded the *Dragnet* spoof, *St George and the Dragonet*?

7. In the 1967 revival who played Friday's veteran partner, Officer Bill Gannon?

8. Who starred as Lieutenant Frank Ballinger in the series *M Squad*?

9. For what did the 'M' stand?

10. In which city was *Naked City* set?

11. How many stories were there in the city according to the regular opening announcement?

12. How was Lieutenant Muldoon (John McIntire) written out of the story?

13. Who replaced Muldoon?

14. What was the name of the *Highway Patrol* chief, played by Broderick Crawford, in the series of that title?

15. For which film had Crawford won an Oscar?

Answers on page 82.

Special Forces

In which series did these organisations feature?

1. OSO (later OSI).
2. CI5.
3. SHADO.
4. THRUSH.
5. CONTROL.
6. SI10.
7. Inter-Agency Defence Command.
8. Nemesis.
9. United Federation of Planets.
10. UNIT.
11. IMF.
12. International Rescue.
13. SEKOR.
14. Spectrum.

Answers on page 82.

War Stories

1. *The Winds of War* opened as Hitler was preparing to march into Poland. At which turning point in the war did it end?

2. Who was the US Navy officer (played by Robert Mitchum) who was the central character of *The Winds of War*?

3. He acted as an emissary of the American President, played by Ralph Bellamy. Who was the President?

4. His son Byron (Jan Michael Vincent) was trapped in Poland with an American Jewish girl, Natalie Jastrow. Who played her?

5. *North and South* was seen as TV's answer to which famous movie?

6. With which historical event was *North and South* concerned?

7. Orry Main was the Southern gentleman and George Hazard the Northerner. Where did they meet?

8. Who played them?

9. What role did Robert Mitchum play in *North and South*?

10. Who was the English actress who played Madeline Fabray, the Creole beauty in love with Main?

11. What role did Elizabeth Taylor play?

12. *Holocaust* dealt with the Nazi extermination of Jews. What was the name of the central family (the parents were played by Fritz Weaver and Rosemary Harris)?

13. Which Nazi leader was played by Ian Holm?

14. Who played the war criminal Adolf Eichmann?

15. Who played Erik Dorf, the lawyer who became a sadistic SS major?

Answers on page 82.

Batman

1. By what name was Batman known in everyday life?

2. And what was the name of Robin, the Boy Wonder?

3. Robin was an orphan; how had his parents died?

4. Batman wore a bat emblem on his shirt; what symbol did Robin wear?

5. What was the name of Batman's house?

6. Who was the only person who knew the secret of Batman and Robin?

7. What was the everyday name and occupation of Batgirl (played by Yvonne Craig)?

8. Batman drove the Batmobile; what was Batgirl's transport?

9. Who created the comic strip on which the series was based?

10. Who was the villain played by Frank Gorshin in long johns embroidered with question marks?

11. Who was the character played by Burgess Meredith?

12. Who played the Siren?

13. What reason did Batman – in cowl and cape – give for declining a stageside seat in a disco in the opening episode?

14. Another series derived from a comic strip, which began in the same year as *Batman*, starred Van Williams in the title role. What was it?

15. How did *Batman* come to the rescue of TV-am in 1987?

Answers on page 82.

Cops Of The
Swinging Sixties

1. In which series did the title of every programme begin with the words, 'Who killed . . . '?

2. Who was the federal agent played by Robert Stack in *The Untouchables*?

3. Stack was famed for having given a young star her first screen kiss in the 1939 movie, *First Love*. Who was she?

4. Why were the agents of *The Untouchables* known as 'T-men'?

5. Which famous newspaper columnist narrated *The Untouchables*?

6. Where was Al Capone's second-in-command, Frank Nitti (Bruce Gordon) finally cornered at the end of the series?

7. Who played Inspector Lew Erskine in *The FBI*?

8. Before allowing *The FBI* to be made, the Director of the Bureau had the cast and crew vetted. Who was he?

9. In which series did Gene Barry play a millionaire, party-going, Los Angeles homicide cop?

10. Who had Gene Barry previously played in a Western series?

11. Why was Robert T. Ironside (played by Raymond Burr) confined to a wheelchair?

12. Where did Ironside live?

13. Burr himself bought an island named Naitumba with his earnings. Where is it?

14. What was the title of the series in which Jack Lord played Steve McGarrett?

15. Lord was said to wear the only one on the island. The only what?

Answers on page 83.

Telly Quotes

From which series are these often-repeated quotes?

1. 'I was born in the Bronx, New York, in December of 1941. I've always felt responsible for World War Two. The first thing that I remember liking that liked me back was food.'

2. 'Remember, the wise man walks always with his head bowed, humble like the dust.'

3. 'This is the city, Los Angeles, California. I work here. I carry a badge.'

4. 'You've got big dreams. You want fame. Well, fame costs and right here's where you start paying.'

5. 'Once upon a time there were three girls who went to the police academy and they were each assigned very hazardous duties, but I took them away from all that.'

6. 'Whenever the laws of any state are broken a duly authorised organisation swings into action. It may be called the state police, state troopers, militia, the rangers or . . . '

7. 'This is the landscape of . . . , desert, forest, mountain and plains; it is intense heat, bitter cold, torrential rain, blinding dust, men risking their lives, earning small reward.'

Answers on page 83.

Weirdos

1. On whose work was *The Addams Family* based?

2. What was the name of the 6 ft 9 in tall, harpsichord-playing butler, played by Ted Cassidy, in *The Addams Family*?

3. What was the pet kept by Gomez (John Astin)?

4. Who was the former Hollywood child star who played Uncle Fester?

5. How did Uncle Fester cause light bulbs to glow?

6. What did Pugsley (Ken Weatherwax) keep in his playroom?

7. Into what could Grandpa (Al Lewis) change himself in *The Munsters*?

8. Who was the former Hollywood sex symbol who played the vampirish Lily Munster?

Answers on page 83.

British Investigators

1. What was the physical peculiarity of *Mark Saber*, played by Donald Gray.

2. What was Gray's original role in postwar TV?

3. In *Randall and Hopkirk (Deceased)* who played the ghostly Marty Hopkirk?

4. In *The Adventures of Sherlock Holmes* who played the great detective?

5. Television filmed at the actual place in the Swiss Alps where Holmes appeared to meet his death in a struggle with Moriarty. Where was it?

6. Who succeeded David Burke as Dr Watson?

7. What was Watson's first name?

8. Where was old Baker Street recreated for the series?

Answers on page 83.

Guys And Dolls

1. Who were the husband and wife who created *Supercar*, *Stingray* and *Thunderbirds*?

2. How many Thunderbird machines were there?

3. Which of them was the green freighter with rollers instead of wheels, designed to carry rescue equipment?

4. Which of the Tracy brothers was the oldest and piloted the scout vehicle Thunderbird 1?

5. Who was the bespectacled genius who invented the machines and equipment?

6. Lady Penelope, the organisation's London agent, rode in a futuristic Rolls-Royce. What was its registration number?

7. Who was the reformed safe-blower who was her chauffeur?

8. Who provided the voice of Lady Penelope?

9. Who was the villain who lived in an Eastern temple, and whose eyes lit up when he cast spells?

10. Who are the puppet masters of *Spitting Image*?

11. How was the effigy of Norman Tebbit usually dressed?

12. Which Labour politician was portrayed as splashing his listeners when he spoke?

13. The voices of Mick Jagger and Jimmy Greaves were provided by a comic later famous for the catchphrase, 'Loadsamoney'. His name?

14. What was the first hit song in the series?

15. From what is the skin of the puppets made?

Answers on page 84.

Find The Link

The following series have a common link in an actor or actress. Who are the stars concerned?

1. *Rich Man, Poor Man/Tender is the Night.*

2. *The Big Valley/The Men From Shiloh/The Six Million Dollar Man/The Fall Guy.*

3. *Edward and Mrs Simpson/The Jewel in the Crown.*

4. *Hard Times/Edward the Seventh/Tender is the Night.*

5. *Jennie, Lady Randolph Churchill/Mistral's Daughter.*

6. *Coronation Street/Randall and Hopkirk (Deceased).*

7. *Maverick/The Saint/The Persuaders.*

8. *The Big Valley/The Thorn Birds/The Colbys.*

9. *The Mary Tyler Moore Show/Rich Man, Poor Man/Roots/Lou Grant.*

10. *The Forsyte Saga/The Pallisers.*

11. *The Forsyte Saga/Anna Karenina.*

12. *Maverick/77 Sunset Strip/The Big Valley.*

13. *Mission Impossible/Star Trek.*

14. *The Six Wives of Henry VIII/Edward the Seventh.*

15. *Kojak/Knots Landing.*

16. *Naked City/Wagon Train/The Virginian.*

Answers on page 84.

Cops, Today
And Yesterday

1. *Prescription Murder*, a TV movie of 1967 led to a popular series four years later. Which?

2. What was *Kojak*'s first name?

3. Why did Kojak suck lollipops?

4. Det. Stavros was played by George Savalas, brother of Telly – under what pseudonym?

5. The star of *Columbo* was reckoned to be the highest paid actor on television in 1977. Who was he?

6. Which of the two stars of *Starsky and Hutch* grew a moustache during the course of the series?

7. Which of the two actors followed a parallel career as a singer?

8. What was the name of *Starsky and Hutch*'s informant, played by Antonio Fargas?

9. On which elite Metropolitan Police unit was *The Sweeney* based?

10. What was the name of the character played by John Thaw?

11. Thaw had starred in an earlier series as a different type of policeman. Who did he play?

12. What was the next cop series in which Thaw starred after *The Sweeney*?

13. Who starred as Lt James Dempsey in *Dempsey and Makepeace*?

14. Who did Don Johnson play in *Miami Vice*?

15. What was the title of the rock album Johnson made during production of the series?

Answers on page 84.

Coronation Street

1. Who bought cakes at the corner shop in episode one, emphasising, 'No éclairs'?

2. Why didn't Elsie Tanner change her surname when she married in 1967?

3. Fred Gee, Alf Roberts and Terry Bradshaw bought a greyhound which they tried to keep in the cellar of the Rovers Return. What was its name?

4. Who became the foster parents of two coloured children, Vernon and Lucy Foyle, in 1974?

5. Who was the burglar for whom Eddie Yeats 'cased' houses while cleaning windows?

6. What was the name of the family whose first act, after taking over the corner shop from Maggie Clegg in 1974, was to refuse credit to Hilda Ogden?

7. What names were given to the Barlow twins, born to Valerie and Ken in 1965?

8. News reached the Street in 1970 that a former resident had died with his baby son, Darren, in a car crash in Australia. Who was he?

9. Who went to live with Albert Tatlock in 1969 taking a mynah bird called Kitchener?

10. Who was the Irish actor who played a tailor in *Never Mind the Quality, Feel the Width* and a taxi driver friend of Elsie Tanner in *Coronation Street*?

11. Who kidnapped baby Christopher Hewitt from his pram outside a shop in 1963?

12. When Alf Roberts was mayor of Weatherfield in 1973, who was his mayoress?

13. Who founded the Property Owners and Small Traders Party?

14. Who died of wounds after being shot by two thugs in a wages snatch?

Answers on page 84.

Funny Situations

1. What was the name of the character played by the star in *The Mary Tyler Moore Show*?

2. MTM Enterprises was founded by Mary Tyler Moore to make her own shows and has since produced *Hill Street Blues* and other series. What is the connection between the company's logo and that of MGM?

3. Edward Asner played a TV news director in *The Mary Tyler Moore Show*; later he starred as city editor in his own series. What was it called?

4. Who starred as a widowed landlady in *Phyllis*?

5. Why did Blanche (Rue McClanahan) of *The Golden Girls* take mouth-to-mouth resuscitation classes?

6. For whom did Dorothy (Bea Arthur) complain in *The Golden Girls* that her husband had left her after 38 years of marriage?

7. A series called *You'll Never Get Rich* later became known by the name of its principal character. Who was he?

8. At which university did Richie, Potsie and Ralph study in *Happy Days*?

9. Who was the Edinburgh-born actor who played Mork from the planet Ork in *Happy Days* (and later *Mork and Mindy*)?

10. What did Mork mean by 'Nanu, nanu'?

11. What was the cover job of agent Maxwell Smart in *Get Smart*?

12. In what kind of building were his organisation's head-quarters in *Get Smart*?

13. What did Smart carry in the heel of one shoe?

14. Who played Agent 99 in *Get Smart*?

Answers on page 85.

Here Comes
The Boss

Who were the superiors of the following?

1. *Kojak.*

2. *Starsky and Hutch.*

3. *Dempsey and Makepeace.*

4. *The Sweeney.*

5. *Columbo.*

6. *Department S.*

7. *Mannix.*

8. *M Squad.*

9. *Police Woman.*

10. *The Six Million Dollar Man.*

11. Lucy in *Here's Lucy.*

12. Lucy in *The Lucy Show.*

13. The IMF in *Mission Impossible.*

14. *Amos Burke, Secret Agent.*

15. *The Champions.*

Answers on page 85.

In The Wild

1. *Survival* is the longest running wildlife series. When did it begin?

2. The *Survival* programme, *The Enchanted Isles*, in 1967 had a commentary by Prince Philip and showed the giant tortoises on islands where Charles Darwin found the clues to his theory of evolution. Which islands?

3. Film maker Cindy Buxton made world headlines in 1982 when she and her assistant Annie Price were trapped on a South Atlantic island. By whom?

4. Who was the Californian camerawoman who was trampled to death by elephants while making her first *Survival* film?

5. The second *Survival* programme, filmed in Suffolk, was about avocets. What are they?

6. He was Belgian; his wife was an English blonde. They starred together in *On Safari* programmes in the Fifties. Their names?

7. Who were the German husband and wife underwater explorers of TV in the Fifties?

8. Is Sir David Attenborough older or younger than his film-maker brother Sir Richard?

9. What was the title of the animal series Sir David made in black and white in the Fifties?

10. What was the title of his 1979 series tracing the development of living species?

11. What was his 1984 series about the environment?

12. In which city is the BBC Natural History Unit based?

13. Who was the French naval captain who made award-winning underwater films?

14. What was the name of the ship which served as his studio for the films?

15. What is the underwater breathing aid of which he was one of the inventors?

Answers on page 85.

Behind These Doors

Who lived, or worked, at these addresses?

1. 165 Eaton Place, London.
2. 485 Bonnie Meadow Road, New Rochelle, New York.
3. 698 Sycamore Road, San Pueblo, California.
4. 1164 Morning Glory Circle, West Port, Connecticut.
5. 221B Baker Street, London.
6. 77 Sunset Strip, Hollywood, California.
7. The Double R Bar Ranch, Mineral City.
8. Walnut Grove, Plumb Creek, Minnesota.
9. Mockingbird Heights, 1313 Mockingbird Lane.
10. 518 Crestview Drive, Beverly Hills, California.
11. The Shiloh Ranch, Medicine Bow, Wyoming.
12. Apartment 3B, 623 East 68th Street, New York City.
13. Carlton Hotel, San Francisco.
14. 123 Main Street, Washington DC.
15. 345 Stone Cave Road, Bedrock.

Answers on page 85.

Star Quotes

Who were the stars who said the following when talking about their series?

1. 'I think people like Henry because he was so very human, with weaknesses, yet also a great glamour. All his women expected too much of him and perhaps he expected too much of them.'

2. 'The owner was the most wonderfully rude man I've ever met. He maintained the guests stopped him from running his hotel.'

3. 'I think she's rather a small, birdy lady who is totally unobtrusive. You'd pass her in the village street, but she knows everything that is going on.'

4. 'I'd say, "The first programme is an hour long, and it's about worms," and I could see their eyes glazing over.'

5. 'OK, we were a manufactured group but the chemistry of our learning did create something which has lasted.'

6. 'The show isn't just about being on a stage. It's about kids who have a commitment to achieving a goal . . . Success isn't just money, it's work.'

7. 'The fact that I happened to choose leather for my fighting kit was a pure accident. Cathy led a very active life and skirts were out of the question.'

8. 'I used to approach that witness stand in a different way in every episode.'

Answers on page 86.

The Man From U.N.C.L.E.

1. For what did the letters 'U.N.C.L.E.' stand?

2. What was the name of the agent played by Robert Vaughn?

3. What was his agent's number?

4. Who played agent Illya Kuryakin?

5. Kuryakin started a fashion trend. What was it?

6. What kind of establishment was Del Florio's, behind which U.N.C.L.E. had its headquarters?

7. With what weapons were U.N.C.L.E. agents equipped?

8. Who was the famous writer of spy thrillers who collaborated on the original idea for the series?

9. What was the insidious organisation that U.N.C.L.E. fought?

10. Leo G. Carroll played the agents' boss. What was the character's name?

11. Carroll died before the TV movie *The Return of the Man From U.N.C.L.E.* was made in 1983. Who took over the role of the boss?

12. Who played agent April Dancer, *The Girl from U.N.C.L.E.*?

13. Who played her partner, Mark Slate?

14. In 1972 Robert Vaughn and Nyree Dawn Porter co-starred as crimebusters in a British series. What was its title?

15. In 1972 Vaughn published a book called *Only Victims*. What was it about?

Answers on page 86.

Westerns: Cattlemen and Settlers

1. In which series did the young Clint Eastwood play Rowdy Yates?

2. Who was the star who made his TV debut as Heath, the illegitimate son of Victoria Barkley in *The Big Valley*?

3. Who was the future *Dynasty* star who played Audra in *The Big Valley*?

4. *Wagon Train* was based on a 1950 John Ford movie. What was it called?

5. Robert Horton, who played scout Flint McCullough in *Wagon Train*, later played a cowboy suffering loss of memory – in which series?

6. In *Wagon Train* the pilgrims were going from Missouri to which state?

7. Who was the star who died on location in 1960 during the making of *Wagon Train*?

8. Who replaced him in the role of Chris Hale?

9. Robert Fuller played trail scout Cooper Smith in *Wagon Train*. Who did he play earlier in *Laramie*?

10. *Rawhide* was the story of a cattle drive from San Antonio, Texas, to where?

11. Who played Wishbone, the cook, in *Rawhide*?

12. What was the name of the family in *The High Chaparral*?

13. The name of *The Virginian* (played by James Drury) was never given. What was his job?

14. Doug McClure played the Virginian's wild assistant. By what name was he known?

15. What role was played by Stewart Granger in *The Men From Shiloh*?

Answers on page 86.

Who He?

Name the actors from the information given.

1. Distinguished-looking American soap star, born 1918. Began career as a sports announcer, film debut in *Destination Tokyo*, has undergone heart by-pass surgery.

2. Titled English actor born 1904, great nephew of Dame Ellen Terry. First stage appearance in 1921. Memorable cameo performances in many series including *Brideshead Revisited*.

3. Respected American actor, born 1926, who starred as an editor. Former President of the Screen Actors' Guild, has won seven Emmy awards.

4. English soap star, born 1935. Made his debut as a boy soprano and played a sergeant in a cop series before becoming factory owner in soap.

5. English actor recently working in America. Noted for tough guy parts but has also recorded 14 albums. Married Michelle Dotrice in 1987.

6. English actor born in Birkenhead. A ladies' hairdresser before becoming star of an action series. Now into target shooting and sky-diving.

7. American actor, gold-ornamented star of an action series. He was formerly a wrestling champion, a military policeman and a bodyguard.

8. Suave English actor, born 1927, son of a London policeman. Was a cartoonist and modelled cardies before action series led to international movie stardom.

9. Titled actor – many think Britain's greatest – born 1907, son of a Dorking vicar. Has produced, presented and starred in TV plays.

10. English actor, born Clapham, 1948. As a child starred in TV's *Just William*, went on to tougher roles. Married Rula Lenska in 1987.

Answers on page 86.

Spicy Sagas

1. *Rich Man, Poor Man* first screened in 1975, starred Peter Strauss and Nick Nolte as brothers. Their names?

2. Both pursued the same girl, Julie Prescott. Who played her?

3. One brother was knifed to death. Which?

4. In *The Thorn Birds* Richard Chamberlain played a Catholic priest. What was his name?

5. The priest fell for an Australian girl, Meggie Cleary. Who played her?

6. Who wrote the music for *The Thorn Birds*?

7. Who was the unknown Danish actress chosen from 700 candidates to play the title role in *Princess Daisy*?

8. Who was seen as her father, a polo-playing Russian prince?

9. *In Mistral's Daughter* who played Mistral, the Parisian Painter?

10. Which Spanish painter inspired the character of Mistral?

11. 'Which of you bitches is my mother?' demanded Lili (Phoebe Cates) in *Lace* of an Englishwoman, a French-woman and an American. Which was?

12. Who played King Abdulla of Sydon in *Lace 2*?

13. Why was Helen Junot (Joan Collins) seeking wartime SS Major Carl von Eiderfeld in *Sins*?

14. In *Sins* Joan Collins played Helen Junot; who played her brother Edmund?

15. What accident befell the first screening in Britain of *Hollywood Wives*?

Answers on page 87.

The Prisoner

1. How was the Prisoner rendered unconscious in the opening titles?

2. The Prisoner had no name, only a number, which he refused to acknowledge. What was it?

3. What was the Prisoner's invariable reply when addressed by this number?

4. Every week the person in charge was different but bore the same number. What was the number?

5. In one episode a woman was in charge. Who played her?

6. Every week the Prisoner was heard asking: 'Where am I?' What was the answer he always received?

7. Every week he also asked: 'What do you want?' What was the invariable answer?

8. In which Welsh resort was the series filmed?

9. Who created the resort?

10. Who, or what, was Rover?

11. For what purpose was the Castle in the Village used?

12. What was the emblem of the village?

13. What was usually carried by the mute, midget butler?

14. What was the name of the agent Patrick McGoohan previously played in *Danger Man*?

15. What is the name of *The Prisoner* appreciation society?

Answers on page 87.

Classic Drama

1. Eric Porter and Nyree Dawn Porter played husband and wife Soames and Irene Forsyte in *The Forsyte Saga*? Are they related in real life?

2. Who was the architect Soames Forsyte engaged to build a house in the country, who fell in love with Irene?

3. What were the names of the children of painter Jolyon Forsyte (played by Kenneth More)?

4. What relation was Fleur (played by Susan Hampshire) to Soames?

5. Who was the baronet's son Fleur married?

6. Who wrote the Forsyte novels?

7. Greta Garbo was famous for her playing of *Anna Karenina* in a 1935 film; who played her in the BBC's 1978 serial?

8. Who played Anna's lover, the dashing Count Vronsky?

9. Patrick Allen starred in Dickens' *Hard Times* as a stern father cramming facts into his children, Louisa and Thomas. What was his name?

10. Who played Micawber in the 1975 BBC production of *David Copperfield*, which starred David Yelland in the title role?

11. In which country did the BBC film *War and Peace*, hiring 1,000 local soldiers as extras?

12. Who played Natasha Rostova in *War and Peace*?

13. In the *BBC Shakespeare* series, who was the comic who played Petruchio in *The Taming of the Shrew*?

14. The BBC planned to cast black American actor James Earl Jones as *Othello* but Equity, the actors' union, insisted on a British actor. Who took the part?

15. Who was the burly, untrained character actor and movie star who played Iago in that production?

Answers on page 87.

Catchphrases

Who said – or sang – and in what?

1. Ten-four.
2. Just trying to get at the facts ma'am.
3. Who loves ya baby?
4. Book 'em, Danno.
5. Exterminate, exterminate!
6. Kissy, kissy!
7. I hate you, Butler!
8. Letters, we get letters, we get stacks and stacks of letters.
9. Move 'em on, head 'em up, head 'em up, move 'em on.
10. You bet your sweet bippy.
11. Hi-yo, Silver!
12. *Que?*
13. Yabba Dabba Doo.
14. You ranggg?
15. Oops, sorry about that!

Answers on page 87.

In Costume

1. The star of *Poldark* was a heart-throb of the Seventies. Who was he?

2. *Poldark* opened with the hero, Ross Poldark, returning home from a war. Which war?

3. In which county was *Poldark* set?

4. What was produced in the family mines?

5. What was the name of the villainous family that schemed to acquire Poldark's property?

6. Who directed *Jesus of Nazareth*?

7. In which country was location filming carried out?

8. Who played the adult Christ in *Jesus of Nazareth*?

9. *The Duchess of Duke Street* was based on the life of Rosa Lewis who kept the Cavendish Hotel, but what was she called in the series?

10. Who played her?

11. Who played Capt. James Onedin in *The Onedin Line*?

12. What was the name of his three-masted schooner?

13. What was the theme music of the series?

14. Who played Mrs Onedin?

15. What was the name of the seaman played by Richard Chamberlain in *Shogun*?

Answers on page 88.

Who She?

Name the actresses from the information given.

1. English actress born 1905, died 1983. At 15 was cinema pianist accompanying silent movies. A soap star from 1960 to 1980 and awarded the OBE.

2. English actress born Kashmir, 1946, daughter of a retired Indian Army major. A model before starring in an action series. Once stripped on TV for charity.

3. British actress, star of American soap. Born 1961, daughter of Princess Elizabeth of Yugoslavia. Played Princess Diana in an American series.

4. American soap actress born in Japan in 1950, brought up in Ruislip where her father was serving with the USAF. A former law student and Miss Miami.

5. American sitcom star born in Houston, trained with the Negro Ensemble Company. Changed name after marrying a sportscaster who proposed to her on TV.

6. English star of American soap, born 1933. An agent's daughter, married four times, *Playboy* centrefold at age of 50.

7. English star of American soap, born 1949, suffers from deafness. A prisoner-of-war in *Tenko* before going to Hollywood. Formerly married to John McEnery.

8. English actress, born 1946, granddaughter of a White Russian. A raunchy image despite starring in Shakespeare on TV. Moved to the US in 1984.

9. English actress, born 1946, first woman president of Oxford University drama society, formerly married to Kenneth Cranham. A star of Waugh series.

10. English actress, born 1938, a hit in tongue-in-cheek agent series, went on to stage acclaim. Now mistress of estate in Scotland where she fishes.

Answers on page 88.

Simply Fantastic!

1. In *Space 1999* why was Moonbase Alpha hurled out of orbit and into space?

2. What was the strange power of Maya (Catherine Schell) in *Space 1999*?

3. In *Battlestar Galactica* what were the metallic creatures from which humans were fleeing?

4. What was the name of Commander Adama's pilot son, played by Richard Hatch?

5. What did Cylon warriors say in acknowledgement of orders?

6. In the language of *Galactica* what was a fumarello?

7. How could aliens in human form be identified in *The Invaders*?

8. What happened to them when they were in need of regeneration to retain their human form?

9. Who played David Vincent, the architect on the run?

10. How did the story end?

11. In *UFO* who played Moonbase commander Lt Gay Ellis?

12. *UFO* involved a computer called SID. What did the initials stand for?

13. From which constellation had the alien invaders of Los Angeles in *V* travelled?

14. What was seen when their skin was torn?

15. Who played Diana, the Visitors' second in command?

16. What was the diameter of the Visitors' spaceships?

Answers on page 88.

They Also Served

In which series were these servants seen?

1. Hop Sing, a cook (played by Victor Sen Yung).
2. Kato, an Oriental chauffeur (Bruce Lee).
3. Henry, another Oriental chauffeur (Leon Lontoc).
4. Edward, a footman (Christopher Beeny).
5. Hey Boy and Hey Girl (Kam Tong and Lisa Lu).
6. Rochester, a valet (Eddie Anderson).
7. Aziz, a houseboy (Ishaq Bux).
8. Starr, a hall porter. (John Cater).
9. Ho-John, a Korean houseboy (Patrick Adiarte).
10. Carlton, a doorman (Lorenzo Music).
11. A mute, midget butler (Angelo Muscat).
12. Silas, a ranch servant (Napoleon Whiting).
13. Alfred, a butler (Alan Napier).
14. Thing, a human right hand.
15. Kyrano, a manservant on a Pacific island.

Answers on page 88.

Animal Stars

1. Who was the animal owned successively by Jeff Miller, Timmy Martin and Corey Stuart?

2. Who was the unusual 300 lb friend of Sandy and Bud Ricks?

3. Gene Autry's horse achieved its own TV series. What was it called?

4. What was the name of *The Cisco Kid*'s horse?

5. *Hopalong Cassidy*'s horse was called?

6. Roy Rogers' horse?

7. Marshal Matt Dillon's horse in *Gunsmoke*?

8. Victoria Barkley's horse in *The Big Valley*?

9. What was the animal owned by Joey Newton (played by Bobby Diamond)?

10. What was the name of *The Partridge Family*'s dog?

11. Elly May's dog in *The Beverly Hillbillies*?

12. The Harts' dog in *Hart to Hart*?

13. *The Waltons'* dog?

14. The Ingalls' dog in *Little House on the Prairie*?

15. What was the name of Agent 13 in *Get Smart*?

Answers on page 89.

Where?

In which real or imaginary cities or towns were these series set?

1. *The Untouchables.*

2. *Fame.*

3. *Beacon Hill.*

4. *The Green Hornet.*

5. *Lou Grant.*

6. *77 Sunset Strip.*

7. *Inspector Morse.*

8. *The Sweeney.*

9. *Dynasty.*

10. *Hawaii Five-O.*

11. *Dragnet.*

12. *Batman.*

13. *Banacek.*

14. *The High Chaparral.*

15. *Soap.*

Answers on page 89.

Modern Drama

1. What was the name of the family in *Brideshead Revisited* whose seat was Brideshead Castle?

2. Laurence Olivier played the head of the family; who played his wife?

3. *Brideshead Revisited* was filmed largely at the Yorkshire home of the BBC chairman of the time. What was its name?

4. What was the career in civilian life of Charles Ryder (played by Jeremy Irons)?

5. Anthony Andrews played Lord Sebastian Flyte; what was the name of his teddy bear which he took everywhere?

6. Who wrote *Brideshead Revisited*?

7. What was the profession of Dick Diver, played by Peter Strauss, in *Tender is the Night*?

8. Who co-starred with Strauss as Nicole Warren, whom he married?

9. *Intimate Contact*, in 1987, starred Daniel Massey in the first British drama series dealing with a controversial and topical subject. What was it?

10. He played businessman Clive Gregory. Who played his wife?

11. On whose short stories were the first *Tales of the Unexpected* based?

12. A dancer is seen in the opening titles undulating to the music. What does she wear?

13. In 1976 Laurence Olivier produced and presented a series *The Best Play of* . . . He also appeared, notably as Big Daddy in which play?

14. Who wrote it?

15. Lady Olivier also appeared in one of the plays. What is her stage name?

Answers on page 89.

Star Trek

1. By what name are *Star Trek* fans known?

2. Who created the series?

3. Who played Capt. James T. Kirk?

4. Mr Spock was only half human. What was the other half?

5. What colour was Spock's blood?

6. Complete the introduction to the programmes: 'These are the voyages of the starship 'Enterprise'. Its five year mission: to explore new worlds, to seek out new life and new civilisations . . . '

7. Of which fleet was the 'Enterprise' the largest starship?

8. The 'Enterprise' had a crew of 430. How many decks did it have?

9. What was Warp One?

10. Which two races were the chief adversaries of the explorers?

11. What weapons did the officers carry on their walkabouts?

12. How many pockets were there in their uniforms?

13. What was the name of the Communications Officer played by Nichelle Nichols?

14. Who played Scotty (Engineering Officer Montgomery Scott) who beamed them up?

15. For *Star Trek: the Next Generation* in 1988, Capt. Kirk was replaced by Capt. Picard, played by a British actor. Who?

Answers on page 89.

Going Pop

1. Who became a major recording star through *The Partridge Family*?

2. In the series his mother was played by Shirley Jones. What was her real relationship to him?

3. What was his first hit with *The Partridge Family*?

4. Of which religious sect were Donny and Marie Osmond members?

5. What was the first hit by *The Monkees*, released three days before the first programme was shown?

6. Who was the diminutive English-born member of *The Monkees*?

7. What was Tom Jones' first international hit in 1965?

8. What was his home town?

9. Which lazy-voiced singer once partnered Jerry Lewis in comedy?

10. Which British newspaper columnist was sued for libel by Liberace, who won, after a long court case?

11. What was Liberace's earlier stage name?

12. What did he invite his fans to call him?

13. Which singer born in 1912 had hits including 'Prisoner of Love' and 'It's Impossible'?

14. What was Engelbert Humperdinck's former name?

15. Who is the musical star of films and television who was born Julia Wells?

Answers on page 90.

Spin-Offs

A spin-off is a series which grows out of, or utilises some of the same characters from another. From which series did these spin off?

1. *The Colbys.*
2. *Police Woman.*
3. *Trapper John.*
4. *Bronco.*
5. *Richie Brockelman, Private Eye.*
6. *Laverne and Shirley.*
7. *The Bionic Woman.*
8. *Phyllis.*
9. *Thomas and Sarah.*
10. *A Different World.*
11. *Kate Columbo.*
12. *Tabitha.*
13. *The Men From Shiloh.*
14. *Pardon the Expression.*
15. *Benson.*

Answers on page 90.

The Real World

1. Which is the oldest and which is the youngest of *Panorama*, *This Week* and *World in Action*?

2. In 1984 *World in Action* persuaded a Conservative MP to join the ranks of the unemployed for a week; he later quit politics and became presenter of *Weekend World*. Who is he?

3. Who has spoken, unseen, most of *World in Action*'s commentaries but is a well-known face in programmes including *Food and Drink*?

4. Who was the producer of *The World at War* who went on to become founding chief executive of Channel 4?

5. One witness in *The World at War* was a famous film star who flew Liberators as a brigadier general in the USAF during World War Two. Who was he?

6. Who spoke the commentary of *The World at War*?

7. Who composed the haunting theme music for *The World at War*?

8. Who presented *Civilisation*?

9. His home was a castle in Kent. Which?

10. Who presented *America*, a 13-part history of the United States, in 1972?

11. He is an American citizen, but where was he born?

12. Dr Bronowski presented *The Ascent of Man*. What was his first name?

13. In which country was he born?

14. As a scientist, what was his best known area of research?

15. Which series has concerned the vanishing way of life of tribes threatened by the advance of civilisation?

Answers on page 90.

Also Known As . . .

These people changed their names – understandably – and found fame. Who did they become?

1. Ruby Stevens.

2. James Lablanche Stewart.

3. Hugh Krampke.

4. Michael Orowitz.

5. Bernard Schwarz.

6. Robert Modini.

7. Angeline Brown.

8. John Joseph Ryan.

9. Kreker Ohanian.

10. David Solberg.

11. Vincento Eduardo Zoine.

12. John Charlton Carter.

13. Peggy Middleton.

14. Orton Hungerford.

15. Eugene Klass.

Answers on page 90.

Superheroes

1. George Reeves was the *Superman* of the Fifties. How did he die?

2. On which newspaper did Clark Kent work in *Superman*?

3. On which uncharted island was *Wonder Woman*'s home?

4. Who was Wonder Woman's mother?

5. What name did Wonder Woman assume in America?

6. Who played Steve Trevor, the American fighter pilot she befriended?

7. Who played the title role in *Buck Rogers in the 25th Century*?

8. In that series Buck returned to earth after 500 years. How had he survived?

9. Buck found a nuclear holocaust had wiped out most of civilisation beyond one enormous computer-governed city. Outside it was a desolate no man's land – known as what?

10. Erin Gray played the blonde commander of Earth's defences who told Buck: 'Deviate from my orders Captain and you'll be blown to a thousand vapours.' What was her name?

11. *The Incredible Hulk* was a Jekyll and Hyde story. What was the name of the doctor played by Bill Bixby?

12. The doctor's predicament was caused by an overdose during an experiment on human strength. An overdose of what?

13. Who was the former Mr Universe who played the Hulk?

14. Britt Reid, otherwise *The Green Hornet*, was claimed to be the great-grandson of a famous Western character. Which?

15. Which series featured a computer named Dr Theopolis and a small robot known as Twiki?

Answers on page 91.

In Which Year?

When did these series begin? In brackets are other events of the same years.

1. *The Professionals* (it was the Queen's Silver Jubilee year and Laker's Skytrain was airborne).

2. *On the Buses* (colour came to ITV and BBC1; man landed on the moon).

3. *The Prisoner* (*News at Ten* started; Dr Barnard performed the first heart transplant).

4. *The World at War* (Princess Anne married: Britain and Iceland fought the cod war).

5. *Coronation Street* (Prince Andrew was born; Princess Margaret married).

6. *The Avengers* (Yuri Gagarin became the first spaceman; the Berlin wall was built).

7. *The Adventures of Robin Hood* (ITV started; Eden succeeded Churchill as Prime Minister).

8. *Jennie* (the three-day working week in Britain; President Nixon resigned in the USA).

9. *Miami Vice* (miners went on strike; Torvill and Dean won Olympic gold).

10. *The Sweeney* (South Vietnam fell; Mrs Thatcher became Conservative leader).

11. *Edward and Mrs Simpson* (publication of *The Times* was suspended; the first test tube baby was born).

12. *The Saint* (Marilyn Monroe died; crisis over missiles in Cuba).

13. *Upstairs, Downstairs* (decimal coinage arrived; the Open University started).

14. *Dr Who* (Lord Home became Prime Minister; President Kennedy assassinated).

Answers on page 91.

Westerns: Lawmen And Law-Breakers

1. What type of gun was used by Hugh O'Brian in the title role of *The Life and Legend of Wyatt Earp*?

2. Where was the controversial gunfight in which Earp, his brothers and Doc Holliday defeated the Clanton gang?

3. Who was the Western movie star who turned down the part of Marshal Matt Dillon in *Gunsmoke* but recommended his protégé, James Arness, who got it?

4. Of which town was Dillon the marshal?

5. Who was Dillon's lame deputy, played by Dennis Weaver?

6. What was the name of the saloon that featured in the series?

7. *Gunsmoke* was the longest-running TV Western; how many years was it in production?

8. Which star of Western series later found religion and became an itinerant preacher?

9. What was the series in which Richard Boone played a hired gun whose visiting cards read; 'Wire Paladin, San Francisco'?

10. What was Paladin's trademark, the emblem on his holster?

11. When James Garner was Bret, who was Bart?

12. Who played Beau Maverick, their British cousin?

13. What were the first names of Smith and Jones, the former Jed 'Kid' Curry and Hannibal Hayes, in *Alias Smith and Jones*?

14. Who was the star of *Alias Smith and Jones* who committed suicide in 1971 by shooting himself beneath a Christmas tree in his home?

15. Why was the character of Bronco Layne introduced into *Cheyenne*?

Answers on page 91.

Dr Who

1. What article of clothing do fans wear in imitation of the Doctor?

2. Who was the first actor to play the Doctor?

3. Two actors who played the Doctor bore the same surname. Who were they?

4. Which actor who played the Doctor later became famous as a TV scarecrow?

5. When did Richard Hurndall play *Dr Who* on TV?

6. Who played the Doctor in the cinema movies in 1965 and 1966?

7. Which actor who played the Doctor collapsed and died at a *Dr Who* convention in Georgia in 1987?

8. What does the Doctor's transporter, the TARDIS, appear to be from the outside?

9. What does the acronym TARDIS stand for?

10. What was the name of the army colonel, played by Nicholas Courtney, who featured in many episodes?

11. Earthlings have one each; the Doctor has two – of what?

12. Which actor, now dead, played the Doctor's long-standing foe, the Master?

13. Who or what were the Urbankans?

14. What was the name of the metallic dog that featured in a number of episodes?

15. Who was the creator of the Daleks?

Answers on page 91.

Fun In The Family

1. Desi Arnaz played the bandleader husband of Lucille Ball in *I Love Lucy* – and was her real husband at the time. In which country was he born?

2. What was the name of the company which Lucille Ball and Desi Arnaz founded to make *I Love Lucy* and which became a Hollywood giant?

3. She was Lucy Ricardo in *I Love Lucy* and Lucille Carter in *Here's Lucy*. Who was she in *The Lucy Show*?

4. In *The Dick Van Dyke Show* the star played writer Rob Petrie. Who played Petrie's wife Laura?

5. The daughter of a Hollywood film star had the leading role of Samantha in *Bewitched*. Who was she?

6. How did Samantha Stevens go about casting a spell in *Bewitched*?

7. What was the name of the daughter of Darrin and Samantha Stevens in *Bewitched* (later the subject of another series)?

8. What is the profession of Cliff Huxtable (Bill Cosby) in *The Cosby Show*?

9. And what is the profession of his wife?

10. How many children have they?

11. *Soap* concerned the families of two sisters. The younger was Mary Campbell; who was the older?

12. What did Mary Campbell say when she surprised her gay son trying on her clothes?

13. A butler, played by Robert Guillaume, later starred in his own series, *Benson*. For whom did he go to buttle in that?

14. How did Granny (Irene Ryan) fall foul of a local doctor in *The Beverly Hillbillies*?

15. How did *The Beverly Hillbillies* refer to their swimming pool?

Answers on page 92.

Jumbled Names

Rearrange the letters to make the names of TV stars.

1. Jane Gommes.
2. Bruno Haigh.
3. Roger Bengus.
4. Tad Mawes.
5. Ben Rossili.
6. Ronny Jascoe.

7. Dana Silven.
8. Laddy Rogan.
9. Monty Chardan.
10. Peter Corri.
11. Rose Peddis.
12. Ron Wanda.

Answers on page 92.

Who They?

1. English actor, born 1945 to a stockbroking family. A star of *The Duchess of Duke Street* before joining a Hollywood soap.

2. English actor, born Bradford, 1934, son of theatrical couple. Many films and TV series including one as a king in 1975. Awarded CBE. Married Prunella Scales.

3. American singer, born 1917, star of stage and film musicals including *Oklahoma!* and *Kiss Me Kate*, who went on to star in a soap.

4. English actress, born 1957, niece of Earl of Dudley. A former model, co-starred with Burt Reynolds in a movie, and married Bryan Brown.

5. English actress, born 1954, won 'Prettiest teenager in England' prize at 16, then *Upstairs, Downstairs* led to Hollywood series. Three times married.

Answers on page 92.

Wheels

What makes of cars were used by the following?

1. James Garner in *The Rockford Files*.
2. Roger Moore in *The Saint*.
3. Edward Woodward in *The Equalizer*.
4. Patrick McGoohan in *The Prisoner*.
5. Gene Barry in *Burke's Law*.
6. Martin Milner and George Maharis in *Route 66*.
7. Steve Forrest in *The Baron*.
8. Dave Starsky in *Starsky and Hutch*.

Answers on page 92.

Weaponry

1. What sort of bullets did *The Lone Ranger* use?
2. What was the Hornet Sting used by *The Green Hornet*?
3. Who had a bracelet that deflected bullets and a lasso that made captives tell the truth?
4. What type of weapons carried by the Starship 'Enterprise' in *Star Trek* contained matter and anti-matter, and could be used as torpedoes or depth charges?
5. With what were the Klingons armed in *Star Trek*?

Answers on page 92.

Cartoon Capers

1. Who were the two men who created *The Flintstones*?

2. In the Thirties they had drawn a famous cat and mouse team for the cinema. What were the names of the animals?

3. What were the first names of Mr and Mrs Flintstone?

4. What was the name of their local newspaper?

5. What kind of roof had their convertible car?

6. What did they use for a vacuum cleaner?

7. For what purpose did they use a lizard with a buck tooth?

8. Who were their neighbours?

9. What was the name of the Flintstones' daughter?

10. Who was her friend, the son of the Flintstones' neighbours, who appeared with her in *The Flintstone Kids*?

11. The same cartoon team created *Yogi Bear*, who lived in which national park?

12. What was his main preoccupation, for which the park ranger kept him under surveillance?

13. What breed of dog was *Scooby-Doo*?

14. In *The Peter Potamus Show* what were Breezely and Sneezely?

15. Who was the voice of Huckleberry Hound, Yogi Bear and Peter Potamus?

Answers on page 93.

Upstairs, Downstairs

1. What was the name of the family that lived upstairs?

2. Who was the co-creator of the series who played Rose Buck, the lady's maid?

3. What was the rarely used first name of Hudson, the butler?

4. What was the fate of Lady Marjorie?

5. Who played Mrs Bridges, the cook?

6. Who played James, the dashing son of the house?

7. Whom did he marry?

8. How did he die?

9. What was the job of Frederick Norton (Gareth Hunt) before becoming a footman at the house?

10. Who played Ruby, the put-upon kitchen maid?

11. Which of the family became a front-line nurse in World War One?

12. Hudson was rejected by the forces. What was his war work?

13. Who played the Welsh chauffeur who married Sarah, the parlourmaid?

14. An American imitation of the series was set in Boston. What was it called?

15. Producer John Hawkesworth went on to make another 'upstairs, downstairs' series in 1976, set in an Edwardian hotel. What was the series?

Answers on page 93.

Women Against Crime

1. Sharon Gless was the third actress to play Christine Cagney of *Cagney and Lacey*; she took over the role from Meg Foster, but who was the first to play the part – in a TV movie?

2. Who was the author who created Miss Marple?

3. What is Miss Marple's first name?

4. What is the name of her village?

5. Who starred in the BBC series which began in 1984.

6. What was the first name of Sgt Makepeace, played by Glynis Barber in *Dempsey and Makepeace*?

7. In which country was Glynis Barber born?

8. Jaclyn Smith was the only one of the three actresses in *Charlie's Angels* to remain to the end. Who was the Angel she played?

9. What was the name of Maddie Hayes' firm in *Moonlighting*?

10. What was the name of the author played by Angela Lansbury in *Murder, She Wrote*?

11. Where did she live?

12. What was the title of her first mystery story to be published?

13. In *Hart to Hart* what was the first name of Mrs Hart?

14. Who starred as *Kate Columbo*, wife of Lt Columbo?

15. A British fan club is known as CLASS. Which series do they support?

Answers on page 93.

Doctors And Lawyers

1. Who played *Dr Kildare* on television?

2. Who played Kildare's elderly mentor, Dr Leonard Gillespie.

3. Who played Kildare most often in the movies?

4. What was the name of the hospital where Kildare worked?

5. What was the medical speciality of *Ben Casey*?

6. Casey's mentor was played by Sam Jaffe; what was his name?

5. Who played Marcus Welby MD?

8. How did his assistant, Dr Steven Kiley (James Brolin) travel on his calls?

9. Who was Marcus Welby's office nurse (played by Elena Verdugo)?

10. Who was the novelist who created Perry Mason?

11. This author appeared in the last episode of Mason: *The Case of the Final Fade-out* in 1966. What role did he play?

12. What was the name of the private eye (played by William Hopper) that Mason employed?

13. Who played Mason in a revival, *The New Adventures of Perry Mason* in 1973?

14. In *The Defenders*, Robert Reed played defence lawyer Kenneth Preston; who played his father and partner, Lawrence?

15. Who wrote the story on which *The Defenders* was based?

Answers on page 93.

Real Lives

1. Of which series about a 19th century royal mistress did Prince Charles reportedly say: 'It was like watching royal home movies'?

2. Who played the king in *The Six Wives of Henry VIII*?

3. Who played Anne Boleyn?

4. Who played the title role in *Elizabeth R*?

5. *Jennie, Lady Randolph Churchill* starred Lee Remick as the American mother of Sir Winston. What was her maiden name?

6. Timothy West played *Edward the Seventh*; who played Queen Victoria?

7. In *Edward and Mrs Simpson*, Edward Fox played the King; who played Mrs Simpson?

8. What was the name of the King's Berkshire retreat where they courted?

9. The series climaxed with the abdication; in what year did Edward abdicate?

10. *Kennedy* was first shown on the 20th anniversary of the assassination of the President. What surprised Americans about the company that made it?

11. Who played John F. Kennedy?

12. Who played the First Lady, Jacqueline Kennedy?

13. *The Last Place on Earth* in 1985 re-examined the story of a British Antarctic explorer. Which?

14. Who played him on screen?

15. *Lillie* was the story of actress Lillie Langtry (played by Francesca Annis). What was the nickname by which she was popularly known?

Answers on page 94.

M*A*S*H

1. For what did the acronym MASH stand?

2. What was the unit's number?

3. In which country was the story set, and what years did it span?

4. Who was the only regular member of the cast who had also been in the 1970 movie, and what was his role?

5. William Christopher played the company priest. What was his name?

6. What were the first names of Capt. Pierce (played by Alan Alda)?

7. How did Corporal Maxwell Klinger (Jamie Farr) try to get his discharge?

8. At the end Klinger decided to stay on and marry. What was the girl's name?

9. What unusual powers did Corporal Radar O'Reilly possess?

10. Whom did the snobbish Major Charles Emerson Winchester III (David Ogden Stiers) replace?

11. Major Winchester accepted the surrender of a group of Chinese soldiers and discovered they had a common interest. What did he teach them?

12. What was the job of Ugly John (played by John Orchard)?

13. Who did Colonel Sherman Potter replace as CO?

14. Who started for home and demobilisation but was brought back when the unit was unable to find a replacement surgeon to deal with a rush of casualties?

15. Alan Alda won awards for M*A*S*H in three different categories. What were they?

Answers on page 94.

And The Best Of British

1. Who co-wrote *Fawlty Towers* with John Cleese?

2. What explanation did Basil Fawlty give to guests to explain Manuel's shortcomings?

3. When *Fawlty Towers* was sold to Spanish television what happened to the character of Manuel, the Spanish waiter?

4. What threatened the success of a gourmet evening and sent Fawlty driving to a restaurant to buy cooked food.

5. Why was Sybil Fawlty hospitalised?

6. *Doctor in the House* was inspired by a book of that title. Who was the author?

7. What was the name of the teaching hospital on which it centred?

8. Who starred as Simon Sparrow in the movie of the book?

9. Who starred as Michael Upton in the TV series in 1969?

10. Who was the doctor played by Robin Nedwell?

11. What were the three 'Doctor' series that followed?

12. In *On the Buses* Reg Varney played bus driver Stan Butler. Who played his conductor?

13. Butler's mother was originally played by Cicely Courtneidge but was succeeded by whom?

14. What was the usual route of the bus driven by Butler?

15. What was the name of the bus company for which he worked?

Answers on page 94.

The Muppet Show

1. Before having their own show the Muppets featured in an American-made series designed to prepare small children for school. What was it?

2. What was the name of the 8 ft canary in that series?

3. Who is the puppeteer who created *The Muppets*?

4. Of which two words was 'Muppet' a composite?

5. Where was *The Muppet Show* made?

6. While some giant *Muppets* needed puppeteers inside them, most were of what type?

7. When a puppeteer's right hand was in a Muppet's head moving the mouth what was his left hand doing?

8. What was the name of the amiable but ugly 9 ft giant Muppet?

9. What was the name of the shaggy, piano-played dog?

10. Who was the hooked-beaked stunt artist?

11. Who were the aged hecklers who sat in a box hating every act?

12. What was the name of the American eagle who denounced shows as 'weird'?

13. In the 'Pigs in Space' feature, what was the name of the starship commanded by Capt. Link Heartthrob?

14. What was the name of the later TV series in which Muppet creatures lived below a lighthouse? (The keeper was played by Fulton Mackay.)

15. What was the name of the first Muppet film made for the cinema in 1979?

Answers on page 94.

Soap Bubbles

1. Who wrote the best seller on which *Peyton Place* was based?

2. *Peyton Place* made big stars of two unknowns. Who were they?

3. Larry Hagman (JR in *Dallas*) is the son of which famous musical comedy actress?

4. Who shot JR in 1980?

5. What do the initials 'JR' stand for?

6. Who played Jock Ewing in *Dallas*?

7. When *Dallas* began, Bobby Ewing and Pamela Barnes had just been married. In which city?

8. Who replaced Barbara Bel Geddes as Miss Ellie while the actress was having heart surgery?

9. In which year did *Dynasty* begin?

10. What was originally to be its title?

11. Michael Praed played Prince Michael of which country in *Dynasty*?

12. Stephanie Beacham was invited to play Sable Colby in *The Colbys* after making an impact in the title role of an ITV series. What was it?

13. In *The Colbys*, what did Fallon's husband Jeff say when she told him she had been kidnapped by aliens who bundled her into a space ship that smelled of cinnamon?

14. What was the source of the wealth of the Channing family in *Falcon Crest*?

15. In *Knots Landing*, where was Richard and Laura Avery's son, Daniel, born?

Answers on page 95.

Trusty Aides

For whom, and in which series, did these faithful assistants work?

1. Rico and Lee (played by Nicholas Georgiade and Paul Picerni).

2. Pancho (Leo Carrillo).

3. Max (Lionel Stander).

4. Jim Halloran (James Franciscus).

5. Betty Jones (Lee Meriwether).

6. Stevie Ames (Diana Decker).

7. Della Street (Barbara Hale).

8. Jim Rhodes (Stephen Brooks).

9. Cordelia Winfield (Sue Lloyd).

10. Kazuo Kim (Poncie Ponce).

11. Chester Goode (Dennis Weaver).

12. Danny Williams (James MacArthur).

13. Bobby Crocker (Kevin Dobson).

14. Mark Sanger (Don Michell).

15. Sgt Lewis (Kevin Whately).

Answers on page 95.

Drama The American Way

1. The author of the novel on which *The Waltons* was based also created *Falcon Crest*. What was his name?

2. In which mountains of Virginia was *The Waltons* set?

3. What was the name of the teenage hero, played by Richard Thomas?

4. His mother, Olivia, was later to be seen in *St Elsewhere*. What was the actress's name?

5. Who wrote the novels on which *Little House on the Prairie* was based?

6. What was the name of the township where the Ingalls family lived in *Little House*?

7. Who played Caroline Ingalls, the wife in *Little House*?

8. In *Route 66* the main characters were played by Martin Milner and George Maharis. What were their names?

9. *Route 66* was the main highway between which two cities?

10. In *Roots* Alex Haley traced his ancestry back seven generations, to a man born in the Gambia who was captured by slave traders and shipped to Georgia. What was his ancestor's name?

11. What was the name of the fighting cock trainer (played by Ben Vereen) who was the first member of the family to be emancipated in 1870?

12. Who played Alex Haley in the sequel *Roots: the New Generation*?

13. Who played an American Nazi in a brief scene in it, giving his fee to charity, and winning an award?

14. What was the name of the book by John Erlichman, jailed after Watergate, upon which *Washington Behind Closed Doors* was based?

15. The President, played by Jason Robards, was based on Richard Nixon, but what was he called?

Answers on page 95.

They're Playing Our Tune

1. Who sang the theme to *The Six Million Dollar Man*?

2. Who provided the music in *Batman*?

3. What was the title of Roy Rogers' theme song?

4. Duane Eddy sang the theme of *Have Gun, Will Travel*. What was it called?

5. What was the theme song of *The Mary Tyler Moore Show*?

6. Richard Chamberlain recorded the theme from *Dr Kildare*. What was it called?

7. Who composed the cornet dirge that is the theme of *Coronation Street*?

8. Who composed the *Dr Who* theme?

9. Who wrote the theme for *The Champions*?

10. Whose orchestra had the biggest hit with the *Dragnet* theme?

Answers on page 95.

The Avengers

1. John Steed's original partner was Dr David Keel, seeking to avenge the murder of his fiancée. Who played him?

2. Honor Blackman was the first *Avengers* girl. What was the name of the character she played?

3. After leaving *The Avengers*, Honor Blackman appeared in the 1964 Bond film, *Goldfinger*. In what role?

4. What was believed to have happened to Peter Peel, husband of Emma (played by Diana Rigg)?

5. Who played Emma Peel's successor, Tara King?

6. Which of Steed's women assistants had a fireman's pole in her flat so that she could slide down to the door?

7. What was the codename of Steed's controller, played by Patrick Newell in a wheelchair?

8. In *The New Avengers* Joanna Lumley played Purdey. From what kind of product was this name taken?

9. What was the career for which Purdey was supposed to have trained?

10. In fact, what was Joanna Lumley's career before she became an actress?

11. What was the name of the character played by Gareth Hunt?

12. Diana Rigg and Joanna Lumley both appeared in a 1969 Bond film. Which?

13. In France *The Avengers* was called *Chapeau Melon et Bottes de Cuir*, meaning, literally, what?

14. Of which famous public school is Patrick Macnee an Old Boy?

15. Brian Clemens, one of the men behind *The Avengers*, went on in 1978 to create a tougher action series noted for its stunts. What was it?

Answers on page 96.

Westerns For The Young

1. What was the name of *The Lone Ranger*, played by Clayton Moore?

2. He was the sole survivor of an ambush – by which gang?

3. Who was the Canadian-born Mohawk who played Tonto in *The Lone Ranger*?

4. Of which tribe of Indians was Tonto a member?

5. 'Kemo sabe' said Tonto, when he addressed the Ranger. What did it mean?

6. Why did Tonto feel indebted to the Ranger?

7. Who starred as *Hopalong Cassidy*?

8. What was the name of Cassidy's ranch?

9. Who wrote the original *Hopalong Cassidy* stories?

10. Roy Rogers called himself King of the Cowboys. Who was his Queen of the West?

11. What was the name of his 'wonder dog'?

12. What was the name of Roy Rogers' singing group?

13. What was the name of Gene Autry's ranch, where in his series he raised horses and walnuts?

14. Who wrote the original short stories on which *The Cisco Kid* was based?

15. Why has *The Cisco Kid* a place in television history?

Answers on page 96.

Black Hearted Villains

1. Who was the Red Chinese criminal (played by Khigh Dhiegh) long sought for by the police in *Hawaii Five-O*?

2. Who was the stowaway spy played by Jonathan Harris in *Lost in Space*?

3. In which series did Chinese agents hypnotise girls at an expensive school with the idea of having them all kill their influential fathers when a signal was given?

4. Who played the Sheriff of Nottingham in *The Adventures of Robin Hood*?

5. Who played Pontius Pilate in *Jesus of Nazareth*?

6. In *The Life and Legend of Wyatt Earp* Trevor Bardette played Earp's great enemy; who was he?

7. How did Alexis, the first Mrs Blake Carrington, cause Krystle, Blake's second wife, to lose the baby she was expecting in *Dynasty*?

8. Who was the crook in *Batman* who tried to spit-roast the Caped Crusader and Boy Wonder on an outsize grill?

9. Who played Al Capone in *The Untouchables*?

10. How did Police Superintendant Ronald Merrick interrogate Hari Kumar in *The Jewel in the Crown*?

11. SS Chief Heinrich Himmler figured in *Holocaust*. At the end of the war he tried to slip through British lines and was arrested. How did he die?

12. Who was the cruel stepfather of *David Copperfield*?

13. Who was the character played by William Smith in *Rich Man, Poor Man*, who set out to destroy the Jordache brothers?

Answers on page 96.

Answers

OPENERS

1. *Callan*.
2. Kitty Russell (played Amanda Blake) of the Longbranch saloon.
3. Sgt Dennis Becker.
4. Superman.
5. The batusi.
6. Joan Collins of *Dynasty*.
7. John Grainger (Charles Bickford).
8. 1968.
9. Germany.
10. Angie Dickinson of *Police Woman*.
11. Bet Lynch (Julie Goodyear).
12. The Bloop.
13. 1984.
14. *The A-Team*.

LAUGHTERMAKERS

1. It was half an hour after lights-out.
2. Alfred Hawthorne Hill.
3. *Who Done It?*
4. Hill's Angels.
5. Violin.
6. Stinginess.
7. Gracie Allen.
8. Dan Rowan.
9. Lily Tomlin.
10. Arte Johnson.
11. Judy Carne.
12. 'This is beautiful downtown Burbank.'
13. *It'll be Alright on the Night*.
14. Blooper shows.
15. Frank Muir.

SECRET AGENTS

1. A tennis player and his coach.
2. Disguise.
3. Cinnamon Carter.
4. 'This tape will self-destruct in five seconds.'
5. Alexandra Bastedo.
6. By mysterious rescuers after a plane crash in Tibet.
7. They could not achieve anything that someone somewhere had not already achieved.
8. *Jason King*.
9. Mark Caine.
10. *Cyborg*.
11. Steve Austin.
12. His legs, one arm and one eye.
13. Jaime Sommers.
14. Gordon Jackson.
15. *Who Dares Wins*.

BONANZA

1. Lorne Greene.
2. Canadian.
3. Three.
4. They were half-brothers. (They had different mothers.)
5. Pernell Roberts.
6. Dan Blocker.
7. Michael Landon (in *Little House on the Prairie*).
8. Eric.
9. 'Candy' Canaday, the ranch foreman.
10. Ponderosa.
11. Virginia City.
12. Silver.
13. Elizabeth, Inger and Marie, Ben's wives (seen in flashbacks).
14. Cochise.
15. *The Big Valley*.

TROUBLE SHOOTERS

1. Simon Templar.
2. ST1.
3. Chief Insp. Claud Eustace Teal.
4. Ian Ogilvy.
5. John Mannering.
6. Antiques.
7. Dana Andrews.
8. John Creasey (originally under the name Anthony Morton).
9. McGill.
10. Lord Brett Sinclair.
11. Tony Curtis.
12. Gene Barry.
13. Colt Seavers.
14. Bad Attitude.
15. Flying.
16. Robert McCall.

NICKNAMES

1. Warren Weber in *Happy Days*.
2. Amy Amanda Allen in *The A-Team*.
3. Sgt Suzanne Anderson in *Police Woman*.
4. Gerald Lloyd Kookson III in *77 Sunset Strip*.
5. Arthur Fonzarelli in *Happy Days*.
6. Col. John Hall in *Sgt Bilko*.
7. Capt. Benjamin Pierce in *M*A*S*H*.
8. Major Margaret Houlihan in *M*A*S*H*.
9. Templeton Peck in *The A-Team*.
10. Commander Henry in *The Winds of War*.
11. Willard Barnes in *Dallas*.
12. Jim Buckley in *Maverick*.
13. Dr Leonard McCoy in *Star Trek*.
14. Aloysius Murphy in *Coronation Street*.
15. Joseph Rockford in *The Rockford Files*.

AUTHOR! AUTHOR!

1. Colleen McCullough.
2. Judith Krantz.
3. Shirley Conran.
4. Judith Gould.
5. Jackie Collins.
6. Arthur Hailey.
7. Leslie Charteris.
8. Robert Ludlum.
9. Harold Robbins.
10. Howard Fast.
11. Herman Wouk.
12. John Jakes.
13. James Clavell.
14. Anthony Trollope.
15. Leo Tolstoy.
16. F. Scott Fitzgerald.
17. Winston Graham.
18. Norman Bogner.
19. Irwin Shaw.
20. Taylor Caldwell.

AMERICAN PEEPERS

1. Thomas Banacek in *Banacek*.
2. Matt Dillon in *Gunsmoke*.
3. His knees.
4. In a biscuit jar.
5. The Korean War.
6. John Forsythe.
7. Intertect.
8. Thomas Sullivan.
9. Possessing cocaine.
10. Journalist.
11. Nick and Nora Charles.
12. *Kookie, Kookie, Lend Me Your Comb*.
13. Dean Martin's.

TALES OF THE RAJ

1. Ben Cross.
2. The Corps of Guides.
3. Anjuli.
4. M. M. Kaye.
5. Daphne Manners.
6. Bibighar.
7. Reporter for *The Mayapore Gazette*.
8. Sister Ludmila.
9. Barbie Batchelor.
10. Ronald Merrick.
11. Sgt in army intelligence.
12. Chillingborough.
13. Wazir, or Chief Minister, to the Nawab of Mirat.
14. Sophie.
15. Paul Scott.

THE FUGITIVE

1. Dr Richard Kimble.
2. Victor Hugo's *Les Misérables*.
3. Death.
4. The train taking him to the penitentiary for execution was derailed.
5. Helen.
6. Philip Gerard.
7. A married sister, Donna Kimble Taft.
8. Four years.
9. They were all aliases used by Kimble.
10. William Conrad narrated both series.
11. Gerard arrived and shot the one-armed man as he was about to push Kimble to his death.
12. Fred Johnson.
13. Orwell.
14. *The Adventurer*.
15. *The Invaders*.

LEGENDARY HEROES

1. Richard Greene.
2. Will Scarlet.
3. Bernadette O'Farrell and Patricia Driscoll.
4. Knotted string sprayed with silver paint.
5. Dick James.
6. *The Legend of Robin Hood*.
7. *Robin of Sherwood*.
8. William Russell.
9. Lord Greystoke.
10. Ron Ely.
11. Cheetah.
12. Jai.
13. Edgar Rice Burroughs.
14. Kwai Chang Caine.
15. *Shane*.

KOOKIE TALK

1. From another town.
2. Ill.
3. Aspirin.
4. Sleep.
5. Advertising men.
6. Getting nowhere.
7. Stop.
8. Let's go.
9. Watch out.
10. Good.
11. Earning money.
12. Horse racing enthusiast.
13. Photograph.
14. Have a fish dinner.
15. Extra chips.

THE FIRST TV COPS

1. Jack Webb.
2. 714.
3. Los Angeles.
4. 'To protect the innocent.'
5. One in every four programmes.
6. Stan Freberg.
7. Harry Morgan.
8. Lee Marvin.
9. Murder.
10. New York.
11. Eight million.
12. The police car in which he was travelling was in a crash with a petrol tanker during a chase and both vehicles exploded.
13. Lt Mike Parker (Horace MacMahon).
14. Dan Mathews.
15. *All the King's Men.*

SPECIAL FORCES

1. *The Six Million Dollar Man.*
2. *The Professionals.*
3. *UFO.*
4. *The Man From U.N.C.L.E..*
5. *Get Smart.*
6. *Dempsey and Makepeace.*
7. *Wonder Woman.*
8. *The Champions.*
9. *Star Trek.*
10. *Dr Who.*
11. *Mission Impossible.*
12. *Thunderbirds.*
13. *Amos Burke, Secret Agent.*
14. *Captain Scarlet and the Mysterons.*

WAR STORIES

1. After Pearl Harbor in December 1941.
2. Commander Pug Henry.
3. Franklin D. Roosevelt.
4. Ali MacGraw.
5. *Gone with the Wind.*
6. The American Civil War.
7. West Point military academy.
8. Patrick Swayze and James Read.
9. An army surgeon.
10. Lesley-Anne Down.
11. Madame Conti, owner of a New Orleans bawdy house.
12. Weiss.
13. Heinrich Himmler.
14. Tom Bell.
15. Michael Moriarty.

BATMAN

1. Bruce Wayne.
2. Dick Grayson.
3. Performing a circus highwire act.
4. R.
5. Wayne Manor.
6. Alfred the butler, played by Alan Napier.
7. She was librarian Barbara Gordon, daughter of the Police Commissioner.
8. The Batcycle.
9. Bob Kane.
10. The Riddler.
11. The Penguin.
12. Joan Collins.
13. 'No thank you, I don't want to be conspicuous.'
14. *The Green Hornet.*
15. *Batman* was screened daily during a technicians' strike – and increased audiences.

COPS OF THE SWINGING SIXTIES

1. *Burke's Law*.
2. Eliot Ness.
3. Deanna Durbin.
4. They worked for the US Treasury.
5. Walter Winchell.
6. In a railway tunnel.
7. Efrem Zimbalist Jr.
8. J Edgar Hoover.
9. *Burke's Law*.
10. Bat Masterson.
11. He was paralysed after being shot.
12. In the attic of police headquarters.
13. One of the Fiji islands in the Pacific.
14. *Hawaii Five-O*.
15. Blue business suit.

WEIRDOS

1. *New Yorker* cartoonist Charles Addams.
2. Lurch.
3. An octopus named Aristotle.
4. Jackie Coogan.
5. By putting them in his mouth.
6. A gallows and an electric chair.
7. A bat.
8. Yvonne De Carlo.

TELLY QUOTES

1. Rhoda Morganstern opening *Rhoda*.
2. Master Teh to Caine in *Kung Fu*.
3. Joe Friday in *Dragnet*.
4. Lydia Grant in *Fame*.
5. Charlie in *Charlie's Angels*.
6. Opening announcement of *Highway Patrol*.
7. Opening announcement of *Rawhide*.

BRITISH INVESTIGATORS

1. He had one arm.
2. A BBC TV announcer.
3. Kenneth Cope.
4. Jeremy Brett.
5. The Reichenbach Falls.
6. Edward Hardwicke.
7. John.
8. Manchester.

GUYS AND DOLLS

1. Gerry and Sylvia Anderson.
2. Five.
3. Thunderbird 2.
4. Scott.
5. Brains.
6. FAB1.
7. Parker.
8. Sylvia Anderson.
9. The Hood.
10. Peter Fluck and Roger Law.
11. In leather bomber jacket and jeans.
12. Roy Hattersley.
13. Harry Enfield.
14. 'The Chicken Song.'
15. Latex.

COPS, TODAY AND YESTERDAY

1. *Columbo.*
2. Theo.
3. To avoid smoking.
4. Demosthenes.
5. Peter Falk.
6. Hutch (David Soul).
7. David Soul.
8. Huggy Bear.
9. The Flying Squad.
10. Jack Regan.
11. Sgt John Mann of the Royal Military Police Special Investigation Branch in *Redcap.*
12. *Inspector Morse.*
13. Michael Brandon.
14. Sonny Crockett.
15. *Heartbeat.*

FIND THE LINK

1. Peter Strauss.
2. Lee Majors.
3. Dame Peggy Ashcroft.
4. Timothy West.
5. Lee Remick.
6. Kenneth Cope.
7. Roger Moore.
8. Barbara Stanwyck.
9. Ed Asner.
10. Susan Hampshire.
11. Eric Porter.
12. Richard Long.
13. Leonard Nimoy.
14. Annette Crosbie.
15. Kevin Dobson.
16. John McIntyre.

CORONATION STREET

1. Ena Sharples.
2. Because the groom's name was also Tanner – Master Sergeant Steve Tanner.
3. Fred's Folly.
4. Ernest and Emily Bishop.
5. Monkey Gibbons.
6. Hopkins (Idris, Vera, Tricia and Granny).
7. Susan and Peter.
8. David Barlow.
9. Alice Pickens.
10. Joe Lynch.
11. Joan Akers.
12. Annie Walker.
13. Leonard Swindley.
14. Ernest Bishop.

FUNNY SITUATIONS

1. Mary Richards.
2. It has a mewing kitten in place of MGM's lion.
3. *Lou Grant*.
4. Cloris Leachman.
5. Because she liked kissing.
6. An air hostess.
7. *Sgt Bilko*.
8. Wisconsin.
9. Robin Williams.
10. Orkan for 'hello'.
11. Greetings card salesman.
12. A music hall.
13. A telephone.
14. Barbara Feldon.

BEHIND THESE DOORS

1. The Bellamys in *Upstairs, Downstairs*.
2. Rob Petrie in *The Dick Van Dyke Show*.
3. *The Partridge Family*.
4. The Stevens in *Bewitched*.
5. Sherlock Holmes.
6. Stuart Bailey and Jeff Spencer in *77 Sunset Strip*.
7. Roy Rogers and Dale Evans in *The Roy Rogers Show*.
8. The Ingalls family in *Little House on the Prairie*.
9. *The Munsters*.
10. The Clampett family in *The Beverly Hillbillies*.
11. Henry Garth in *The Virginian*; later Col. Alan Mackenzie in *The Men From Shiloh*.
12. The Ricardos in *I Love Lucy*.
13. Paladin in *Have Gun, Will Travel*.
14. CONTROL in *Get Smart*.
15. *The Flintstones*.

HERE COMES THE BOSS

1. Capt. Frank McNeil (Dan Frazer).
2. Capt. Dobey (Bernie Hamilton).
3. Chief Supt. Gordon Spikings (Ray Smith).
4. Frank Haskins (Garfield Morgan).
5. Capt. Sampson (Bill Zuckert).
6. Sir Curtis Seretse (Dennis Alaba Peters).
7. Lou Wickersham (Joseph Campanella).
8. Capt. Grey (Paul Newlan).
9. Lt Paul Marsh (Val Bisoglio).
10. Oscar Goldman (Richard Anderson).
11. Harrison Otis Carter (Gale Gordon).
12. Theodore J. Mooney (Gale Gordon).
13. Jim Phelps (Peter Graves).
14. 'The Man' (Carl Benton Reid).
15. Commander Tremayne (Anthony Nicholls).

IN THE WILD

1. 1961.
2. The Galapagos.
3. Invading Argentine troops; they were on South Georgia.
4. Lee Lyon.
5. Rare wading birds.
6. Armand and Michaela Denis.
7. Hans and Lotte Hass.
8. Sir David was born in 1926; Sir Richard in 1923.
9. *Zoo Quest*.
10. *Life on Earth*.
11. *The Living Planet*.
12. Bristol.
13. Capt. Jacques-Yves Cousteau.
14. *Calypso*.
15. The aqualung.

STAR QUOTES

1. Keith Michell on *The Six Wives of Henry VIII*.
2. John Cleese on *Fawlty Towers*.
3. Joan Hickson on *Miss Marple*.
4. Sir David Attenborough on *Life on Earth*.
5. Mickey Dolenz on *The Monkees*.
6. Debbie Allen on *Fame*.
7. Honor Blackman on *The Avengers*.
8. Raymond Burr on *Perry Mason*.

WESTERNS: CATTLEMEN AND SETTLERS

1. *Rawhide*.
2. Lee Majors.
3. Linda Evans.
4. *Wagonmaster*.
5. *A Man Called Shenandoah*.
6. California.
7. Ward Bond.
8. John McIntyre.
9. Rancher Jess Harper.
10. Sedalia, Kansas.
11. Paul Brinegar.
12. Cannon.
13. Foreman of the Shiloh ranch.
14. Trampas.
15. Col. Alan MacKenzie.

THE MAN FROM U.N.C.L.E.

1. United Network Command for Law and Enforcement.
2. Napoleon Solo.
3. Eleven.
4. David McCallum.
5. A rollneck sweater instead of a shirt and tie.
6. A tailor's. The agent's entrance was through a changing room.
7. A modified P38 automatic.
8. Ian Fleming, creator of James Bond.
9. THRUSH.
10. Alexander Waverly.
11. Patrick Macnee.
12. Stefanie Powers.
13. Noel Harrison.
14. *The Protectors*.
15. The blacklisting of Hollywood actors and writers by the Un-American Activities Committee.

WHO HE?

1. John Forsythe.
2. Sir John Gielgud.
3. Ed Asner.
4. Johnny Briggs.
5. Edward Woodward.
6. Lewis Collins.
7. Mr T.
8. Roger Moore.
9. Sir Laurence (Lord) Olivier.
10. Dennis Waterman.

SPICY SAGAS

1. Rudy and Tom Jordache.
2. Susan Blakely.
3. Tom (Nick Nolte).
4. Ralph de Bricassart.
5. Rachel Ward.
6. Henry Mancini.
7. Merete Van Kemp.
8. Stacy Keach.
9. Stacy Keach.
10. Picasso.
11. Judy, the American.
12. Anthony Higgins.
13. His troops had caused the death of her mother.
14. Timothy Dalton.
15. The penultimate reel was omitted.

CATCHPHRASES

1. Brod Crawford as Dan Mathews in *Highway Patrol*.
2. Jack Webb as Sgt Joe Friday in *Dragnet*.
3. Telly Savalas in the title role of *Kojak*.
4. Jack Lord as Steve McGarrett in *Hawaii Five-O*.
5. The Daleks in *Dr Who*.
6. Miss Piggy in *The Muppet Show*.
7. Stephen Lewis as bus inspector in *On the Buses*.
8. Girl singers in *The Perry Como Show*.
9. Frankie Laine in *Rawhide*.
10. Dick Martin in *Laugh-In*.
11. Clayton Moore as *The Lone Ranger*.
12. Andrew Sachs as Manuel in *Fawlty Towers*.
13. Fred Flintstone in *The Flintstones*.
14. Ted Cassidy as Lurch, the butler in *The Addams Family*.
15. Don Adams as Maxwell Smart in *Get Smart*.

THE PRISONER

1. By gas through the keyhole of his apartment.
2. No. 6.
3. 'I am not a number; I am a free man.'
4. No. 2.
5. Mary Morris.
6. 'In the Village.'
7. 'Information.'
8. Portmeirion.
9. Sir Clough Williams-Ellis.
10. A plastic balloon which guarded the perimeter and bounded after and enveloped escapees.
11. A hospital and brain-washing centre.
12. A penny-farthing bicycle.
13. An umbrella.
14. John Drake.
15. Six of One.

CLASSIC DRAMA

1. No.
2. Philip Bosinney.
3. Holly and Jolly.
4. Daughter.
5. Michael Mont.
6. John Galsworthy.
7. Nicola Pagett.
8. Stuart Wilson.
9. Thomas Gradgrind.
10. Arthur Lowe.
11. Yugoslavia.
12. Morag Hood.
13. John Cleese.
14. Anthony Hopkins.
15. Bob Hoskins.

IN COSTUME

1. Robin Ellis.
2. American War of Independence.
3. Cornwall.
4. Copper.
5. Warleggan.
6. Franco Zeffirelli.
7. Tunisia.
8. Robert Powell.
9. Louisa Trotter.
10. Gemma Jones.
11. Peter Gilmore.
12. *Charlotte Rhodes*.
13. Khachaturyan's *Spartacus*.
14. Anne Stallybrass.
15. John Blackthorne.

WHO SHE?

1. Violet Carson.
2. Joanna Lumley.
3. Catherine Oxenberg.
4. Victoria Principal.
5. Phylicia Rashad.
6. Joan Collins.
7. Stephanie Beacham.
8. Helen Mirren.
9. Diana Quick.
10. Diana Rigg.

SIMPLY FANTASTIC!

1. A nuclear waste dump on the moon exploded.
2. She could transform herself into any kind of organic matter from a tree to a lion.
3. Cylons.
4. Capt. Apollo.
5. 'By your leave.'
6. A cigar.
7. Their little fingers jutted awkwardly.
8. They began to glow.
9. Roy Thinnes.
10. There was never a concluding episode.
11. Gabrielle Drake.
12. Space Intruder Detector.
13. Sirius.
14. A lizard skin beneath.
15. Jane Badler.
16. Five miles.

THEY ALSO SERVED

1. *Bonanza*.
2. *The Green Hornet*.
3. *Burke's Law*.
4. *Upstairs, Downstairs*.
5. *Have Gun, Will Travel*.
6. *The Jack Benny Programme*.
7. *The Jewel in the Crown*.
8. *The Duchess of Duke Street*.
9. *M*A*S*H*.
10. *Rhoda*.
11. *The Prisoner*.
12. *The Big Valley*.
13. *Batman*.
14. *The Addams Family*.
15. *Thunderbirds*.

ANIMAL STARS

1. Lassie, a collie.
2. Flipper, a dolphin.
3. *Champion, the Wonder Horse*.
4. Diablo.
5. Topper.
6. Trigger.
7. Marshal.
8. Misty Girl.
9. Fury, a black stallion.
10. Simon.
11. Duke.
12. Freeway.
13. Reckless.
14. Jack.
15. Fang.

MODERN DRAMA

1. Marchmain.
2. Claire Bloom.
3. Castle Howard.
4. Painter.
5. Aloysius.
6. Evelyn Waugh.
7. Psychiatrist.
8. Mary Steenburgen.
9. Aids.
10. Claire Bloom.
11. Roald Dahl.
12. A white body stocking and white tights, but she is seen only as a silhouette.
13. *Cat on a Hot Tin Roof*.
14. Tennessee Williams.
15. Joan Plowright.

WHERE?

1. Chicago.
2. New York City.
3. Boston.
4. Washington.
5. Los Angeles.
6. Hollywood.
7. Oxford.
8. London.
9. Denver.
10. Honolulu.
11. Los Angeles.
12. Gotham City.
13. Boston.
14. Tucson, Arizona.
15. Dunn's River, Connecticut.

STAR TREK

1. Trekkies.
2. Gene Roddenberry.
3. William Shatner.
4. Vulcan.
5. Green.
6. 'To boldly go where no man has gone before.'
7. The United Federation of Planets.
8. Eight.
9. The speed of light.
10. Romulans and Klingons.
11. Portable phasers.
12. None.
13. Lt Uhuru.
14. James Doohan.
15. Patrick Stewart.

GOING POP

1. David Cassidy.
2. Stepmother.
3. 'I Think I Love You.'
4. Mormons.
5. 'Last Train to Clarksville.'
6. David Jones.
7. 'It's Not Unusual.'
8. Pontypridd.
9. Dean Martin.
10. Cassandra (William Connor) of the *Daily Mirror*.
11. Walter Busterkeys.
12. Lee.
13. Perry Como.
14. Gerry Dorsey.
15. Julie Andrews.

SPIN-OFFS

1. *Dynasty*.
2. *Police Story*.
3. *M*A*S*H*.
4. *Cheyenne*.
5. *The Rockford Files*.
6. *Happy Days*.
7. *The Six Million Dollar Man*.
8. *The Mary Tyler Moore Show*.
9. *Upstairs, Downstairs*.
10. *The Cosby Show*.
11. *Columbo*.
12. *Bewitched*.
13. *The Virginian*.
14. *Coronation Street*.
15. *Soap*.

THE REAL WORLD

1. *Panorama* began in 1953, *This Week* in 1956 and *World in Action* in 1963.
2. Matthew Parris.
3. Chris Kelly.
4. Jeremy Isaacs.
5. James Stewart.
6. Laurence Olivier.
7. Carl Davis.
8. Sir Kenneth (later Lord) Clark.
9. Saltwood Castle.
10. Alistair Cooke.
11. Manchester.
12. Jacob.
13. Poland.
14. Smokeless fuels. (He was the National Coal Board's Director of Research.)
15. *Disappearing World*.

ALSO KNOWN AS ...

1. Barbara Stanwyck.
2. Stewart Granger.
3. Hugh O'Brian.
4. Michael Landon.
5. Tony Curtis.
6. Robert Stack.
7. Angie Dickinson.
8. Jack Lord.
9. Mike Connors.
10. David Soul.
11. Vince Edwards.
12. Charlton Heston.
13. Yvonne De Carlo.
14. Ty Hardin.
15. Gene Barry.

SUPERHEROES

1. He shot himself in 1959 because he could not get other roles.
2. *The Daily Planet*.
3. Paradise Island.
4. Queen Hippolyte of the Amazons.
5. Diana Prince.
6. Lyle Waggoner.
7. Gil Gerard.
8. In deep frozen hibernation.
9. Anarchia.
10. Wilma Deering.
11. David Banner.
12. Gamma rays.
13. Lou Ferrigno.
14. The Lone Ranger.
15. *Buck Rogers in the 25th Century*.

IN WHICH YEAR?

1. 1977.
2. 1969.
3. 1967.
4. 1973.
5. 1960.
6. 1961.
7. 1955.
8. 1974.
9. 1984.
10. 1975.
11. 1978.
12. 1962.
13. 1971.
14. 1963.

WESTERNS: LAWMEN AND LAW-BREAKERS

1. A Buntline Special .45 calibre six-gun.
2. The OK Corral.
3. John Wayne.
4. Dodge City.
5. Chester Goode.
6. The Longbranch.
7. Twenty.
8. Ty Hardin of *Bronco*.
9. *Have Gun, Will Travel*.
10. A white chess knight.
11. Jack Kelly in *Maverick*.
12. Roger Moore.
13. Joshua Smith and Thaddeus Jones.
14. Pete Duel.
15. Clint Walker, the star of *Cheyenne*, was suspended by the studio in a dispute about his contract.

DR WHO

1. Long woollen scarves.
2. William Hartnell.
3. Tom Baker and Colin Baker.
4. Jon Pertwee (in *Worzel Gummidge*).
5. In *The Five Doctors* in 1983, in which he impersonated the late William Hartnell's playing of the Doctor.
6. Peter Cushing.
7. Patrick Troughton.
8. A police box.
9. Time And Relative Dimensions In Space.
10. Lethbridge-Stewart.
11. Hearts.
12. Roger Delgado.
13. A race of frog people.
14. K9.
15. Terry Nation.

FUN IN THE FAMILY

1. Cuba.
2. Desilu.
3. Lucy Carmichael.
4. Mary Tyler Moore.
5. Elizabeth Montgomery.
6. By wrinkling her nose.
7. Tabitha.
8. Obstetrician.
9. Lawyer.
10. Five.
11. Jessica Tate.
12. 'I've told you a hundred times, that dress fastens at the back.'
13. The state governor.
14. By practising mountain remedies.
15. 'The ce-ment pond.'

WHO THEY?

1. Christopher Cazenove.
2. Timothy West.
3. Howard Keel.
4. Rachel Ward.
5. Lesley-Anne Down.

JUMBLED NAMES

1. Gemma Jones.
2. Hugh O'Brian.
3. George Burns.
4. Adam West.
5. Robin Ellis.
6. Jason Connery.
7. Linda Evans.
8. Donald Gray.
9. Cathryn Damon.
10. Eric Porter.
11. Doris Speed.
12. Dan Rowan.

WHEELS

1. Pontiac Firebird.
2. Volvo P1800.
3. Jaguar.
4. Lotus Seven.
5. Rolls-Royce.
6. 1960 Chevrolet.
7. Jensen.
8. Ford.

WEAPONRY

1. Silver (to remind him to shoot sparingly and remember the high cost of human life).
2. It emitted high-pitched sound that could break down doors.
3. *Wonder Woman*.
4. Photon torpedoes.
5. Sonic disrupter pistols.

CARTOON CAPERS

1. William Hanna and Joe Barbera.
2. Tom and Jerry.
3. Fred and Wilma.
4. *The Daily Slate*.
5. Thatched.
6. A baby elephant on roller skates.
7. A tin opener.
8. Barney and Betty Rubble.
9. Pebbles.
10. Bamm Bamm.
11. Jellystone.
12. Acquiring picnickers' lunch baskets.
13. A Great Dane.
14. A polar bear and a seal.
15. Daws Butler.

WOMEN AGAINST CRIME

1. Loretta Swit.
2. Agatha Christie.
3. Jane.
4. St Mary Mead.
5. Joan Hickson.
6. Harriet.
7. South Africa.
8. Kelly Garrett.
9. The Blue Moon Detective Agency.
10. Jessica Fletcher.
11. Cabot Cove, Maine.
12. *The Corpse Danced at Midnight*.
13. Jennifer.
14. Kate Mulgrew.
15. CLASS stands for Cagney and Lacey Appreciation of the Series Society.

UPSTAIRS, DOWNSTAIRS

1. Bellamy.
2. Jean Marsh.
3. Angus.
4. She died in the *Titanic* disaster.
5. Angela Baddeley.
6. Simon Williams.
7. Richard Bellamy's secretary, Hazel (Meg Wynn Owen).
8. He shot himself in the wake of the Wall Street crash.
9. He was James Bellamy's batman in the army.
10. Jenny Tomasin.
11. Lady Georgina Worsley, Bellamy's niece and ward.
12. Special constable.
13. John Alderton.
14. *Beacon Hill*.
15. *The Duchess of Duke Street*.

DOCTORS AND LAWYERS

1. Richard Chamberlain.
2. Raymond Massey.
3. Lew Ayres.
4. Blair General.
5. He was a neurosurgeon.
6. Dr David Zorba.
7. Robert Young.
8. On a motorcycle.
9. Consuelo Lopez.
10. Erle Stanley Gardner.
11. The judge.
12. Paul Drake.
13. Monte Markham.
14. E. G. Marshall.
15. Reginald Rose.

REAL LIVES

1. *Lillie*.
2. Keith Michell.
3. Dorothy Tutin.
4. Glenda Jackson.
5. Jerome.
6. Annette Crosbie.
7. Cynthia Harris.
8. Fort Belvedere.
9. 1936.
10. It was British.
11. Martin Sheen.
12. Blair Brown.
13. Capt. Robert Falcon Scott.
14. Martin Shaw.
15. The Jersey Lily.

M*A*S*H

1. Mobile Army Surgical Hospital.
2. The 4077th
3. Korea, 1950–3.
4. Gary Burghoff as Cpl Radar O'Reilly.
5. Father John Mulcahy.
6. Benjamin Franklin.
7. By dressing in women's clothing.
8. Soon-Lee.
9. Extra-sensory perception (ESP).
10. Major Frank Burns.
11. The common interest was music: he taught them Mozart's quintet for clarinet and strings.
12. Anaesthetist.
13. Col. Henry Blake.
14. Capt. B. J. Hunnicutt.
15. As actor, writer and director.

AND THE BEST OF BRITISH

1. Connie Booth.
2. 'You'll have to excuse him – he comes from Barcelona.'
3. He became Italian.
4. The chef was drunk.
5. An ingrowing toenail.
6. Richard Gordon.
7. St Swithin's.
8. Dirk Bogarde.
9. Barry Evans.
10. Duncan Waring.
11. *Doctor at Sea, Doctor at Large, Doctor on the Go*.
12. Bob Grant.
13. Doris Hare.
14. No. 11 to the cemetery gates.
15. Luxton.

THE MUPPET SHOW

1. *Sesame Street*.
2. Big Bird.
3. Jim Henson.
4. Marionette and puppet.
5. Boreham Wood, Herts.
6. Glove puppets.
7. Moving the puppet's left arm.
8. Sweetums.
9. Rowlf.
10. The Great Gonzo.
11. Statler and Waldorf.
12. Sam.
13. 'Swinetrek'.
14. *Fraggle Rock*.
15. *The Muppet Movie*.

SOAP BUBBLES

1. Grace Metalious.
2. Mia Farrow and Ryan O'Neal.
3. Mary Martin.
4. Kristin Shepard, his mistress (played by Mary Crosby).
5. John Ross.
6. Jim Davis.
7. New Orleans.
8. Donna Reed.
9. 1981.
10. *Oil*.
11. Moldavia.
12. *Connie*.
13. 'Were they baking?'
14. Vineyards in the Napa valley.
15. In the back of their car.

TRUSTY AIDS

1. Eliot Ness in *The Untouchables*.
2. *The Cisco Kid*.
3. The Harts in *Hart to Hart*.
4. Lt Muldoon in *Naked City*.
5. *Barnaby Jones*.
6. *Mark Saber*.
7. *Perry Mason*.
8. Insp. Lew Erskine in *The FBI*.
9. *The Baron*.
10. Tracy Steele and Tom Lopaka in *Hawaiian Eye*.
11. Marshal Matt Dillon in *Gunsmoke*.
12. Steve McGarrett in *Hawaii Five-O*.
13. *Kojak*.
14. *Ironside*.
15. *Inspector Morse*.

DRAMA THE AMERICAN WAY

1. Earl Hamner Jr.
2. Blue Ridge.
3. John-Boy.
4. Michael Learned.
5. Laura Ingalls Wilder.
6. Plumb Creek, Minnesota.
7. Karen Grassle.
8. Todd Stiles and Buzz Murdock.
9. Chicago and Los Angeles.
10. Kunta Kinte.
11. Chicken George.
12. James Earl Jones.
13. Marlon Brando.
14. *The Company*.
15. Richard Monckton.

THEY'RE PLAYING OUR TUNE

1. Dusty Springfield.
2. Nelson Riddle.
3. 'Happy Trails to You.'
4. 'The Ballad of Paladin.'
5. 'Love Is All Around.'
6. 'Three Stars Will Shine Tonight.'
7. Eric Spear.
8. Ron Grainer.
9. Tony Hatch.
10. Ray Anthony.

THE AVENGERS

1. Ian Hendry.
2. Cathy Gale.
3. Pussy Galore.
4. He was believed killed in an air crash in the Amazon jungles (but eventually returned).
5. Linda Thorson.
6. Tara King.
7. Mother.
8. Guns.
9. Ballerina.
10. Model.
11. Mike Gambit.
12. *On Her Majesty's Secret Service*.
13. Bowler Hat and High Leather Boots.
14. Eton.
15. *The Professionals*.

BLACK HEARTED VILLAINS

1. Wo Fat.
2. Col. Zachary Smith.
3. *The Man From U.N.C.L.E.*
4. Alan Wheatley.
5. Rod Steiger.
6. Old Man Clanton, head of the Clanton gang.
7. She 'accidentally' fired a shot while Krystle was riding, causing her horse to bolt.
8. The Minstrel (Van Johnson).
9. Neville Brand.
10. He had him bound, then flogged him.
11. He bit on a phial of cyanide.
12. Edward Murdstone.
13. Bill Falconetti.

WESTERNS FOR THE YOUNG

1. John Reid.
2. The Butch Cavendish Hole in the Wall gang.
3. Jay Silverheels.
4. Potawatomie.
5. Faithful friend.
6. The Lone Ranger had cared for Tonto as a child, after Tonto's family had been killed by renegade Indians.
7. William Boyd.
8. The Bar 20.
9. Clarence E. Mulford.
10. Dale Evans.
11. Bullet.
12. Sons of the Pioneers.
13. Melody.
14. O. Henry.
15. It was the first TV series to be filmed in colour.